the guns 1914-18

I V Hogg

Editor-in-Chief: Barrie Pitt
Editor: David Mason
Art Director: Sarah Kingham
Picture Editor: Robert Hunt
Designer: David A Evans
Cover: Denis Piper
Special Drawings: John Batchelor
Photographic Research: Colette Dumez
Cartographer: Richard Natkiel

First Printing: November 1971
Printed in United States of America

Ballantine Books Inc.
101 Fifth Avenue New York NY 10003

An Intext Publisher

Contents

"Now thrive the armourers..."

Introduction by Barrie Pitt

Although, as its title indicates, this book is mainly concerned with the use of artillery throughout the First World War, it is necessary to go back in time – to the latter part of the 19th Century – in order to find the origins of the rapid advance which was made in the design of guns and to what extent the destructive power of artillery ammunition increased over a comparatively short period.

The Industrial Revolution, with its advancement in engineering techniques. enabled engineers of all kinds to break free from the restrictions imposed by both the limited scope of the materials at their disposal, and the outmoded methods of manufacture then in use. This emancipation brought improved bridges, railways, locomotives, and manufacturing machinery – and in the field of warfare it led firstly to the construction of the ironclad battleship – an armoured and apparently invincible monster, the ultimate in warship design. But every force propagates a counter-force and inevitably the progress in armour-plating battleships stimulated the invention of methods to pierce the armour. Thus it came about that the existence of the new warships played a large part in forcing designers of guns to break with the traditions of the past and begin the evolutionary process which produced the direct ancestors of today's artillery.

This evolutionary process began with the introduction of 'rear-end' loading of guns and continued with the invention of suitable machinery for overcoming the problem of recoil. Both of these design virtues were incorporated in a French field gun – the 75mm Model 1897 – which could be loaded and fired so rapidly that it brought a new term into the vocabulary of ordnance – the 'Quick Firing' or QF gun – and induced in the French military mind ideas for the use of artillery which were to last for many years to come.

As guns improved, it became necessary to improve the ammunition they fired. One of the first developments in the design of shell ammunition was the introduction of piercing shot – the ironclad being in the designer's mind as a likely target – and at the same time shrapnel shells were made infinitely more effective by constructing them so that the bullets expelled by the bursting shell were all made to go in the direction calculated to do most damage. A third development resulted in the explosive or 'common' shell, for use against fortifications or munitions.

And as the improved engineering of the gun demanded new shells, so the better-constructed shell called for an improvement in the explosive which propelled it. Gunpowder, which had served as an explosive medium from Crècy to the Crimea, was no longer acceptable for use with modern weapons.'

To fulfil this need, the chemists invented 'high' and 'low' explosives – the former to fill the shell and the latter to propel it. The British used 'Lyddite' – picric acid melted and cast into the shell, named somewhat obscurely after the Siege Artillery School at Lydd – with 'Cordite' as a propellant. The Germans experimented with trinitrotoluene (TNT) and as Lyddite left much to be desired as a shell-filling, the British eventually followed this example, both countries managing to solve the problem of producing a suitable fuse for exploding this material in time for the beginning of the First World War.

The use of this newly-developed artillery in a major European conflict had, up until the start of the First World War, been a matter for theory and speculation; now the combatants had the opportunity to put theory into practice. The German firm of Krupp – a name even then synonymous with the armament industry – had developed a huge 42cm howitzer which fired an 820-kilogramme shell and which was brought into action for the first time against the Belgian fortified complex of Liège. The enormous shells fell nearly vertically from the top of their trajectories – almost three miles above the surface of the earth – crashing down through the roofs of the forts to explode with devastating effect within them.

Once Liège had fallen, the 42cm battery was moved to Namur, and was joined there by 30.5cm weapons built at the famous Skoda works and sent to the Western Front by the Austro-Hungarian army. The forts at Namur were as powerless to resist the bludgeoning attacks of these giant guns as those of Liège, and soon their dejected garrisons were filing into captivity. They were later joined by the survivors of the garrisons of the forts surrounding Maubeuge in north-east France which were also hammered into submission.

As the war stagnated in 1915 and the Western Front congealed virtually into the line that it was to keep until the Armistice, the fighting soldiers demanded new weapons with which to fight a static war. The Germans produced the *minenwerfer* to be countered by the British-designed Stokes 3-in mortar – the archetype of every mortar built since. When gas became accepted as a front-line weapon, it was only a matter of time before gas-filled shells were being fired from guns as just another type of ammunition – until the British introduced a cheap but effective projector for the silent delivery of gas-filled drums.

When the aeroplane was used for warlike purposes it made inevitable the development of the anti-aircraft gun, which in turn led to the invention of ancillary weapons such as sound locators and searchlights to supplement the work of the guns.

This book is not a catalogue of technical data, a list of esoteric terms dear to the heart of the artillerist, but a lucid account of the history of the gun from its inception in its modern form up to the end of the First World War – from the French 75mm to the Brobdingnagian weapon developed by the Germans to shell Paris.

Master Gunner Ian Hogg takes the non-technical reader by the hand and, without condescension, explains technical matters in terms a layman can understand; and the uses of the weapons he describes so expertly are seen in the context of the war as a whole, for his knowledge is by no means limited to his beloved guns. And as readers of his previous books will know, Ian Hogg is incapable of writing on any subject without introducing a strain of humour which makes his work a delight to read.

The state of the nations

The events which led up to the outbreak of war in August 1914 have been well documented and discussed, and one thing is fairly obvious – that when war came it didn't catch the combatants by surprise. The coming war had been seen from afar, and the armies and navies of Europe had been checking their inventories and exercising their troops well in advance. But what did surprise them was the scope to which it blossomed and the voracious appetite it developed for men and machinery; running through the entire history of the war is the constant struggle for more and more of both. In no field is this more obvious than in the artilleryman's war, for the war of 1914–1918 became an artillery duel of vast proportions. Once the static front was delineated, more and more guns were called into play to hurl defiance across No-Man's Land and to provide protective fires for the infantry's manoeuvres.

But it was for open warfare, mobile warfare, fluid warfare – call it what you like – that the artillerymen of all the combatant countries were trained, because this appeared to be the system of warfare which the 20th Century had produced. So far as the British army was concerned, the strategists could look back to 1854 and the Crimea to see the last positional war; that had been little more than a prolonged and untidy siege action, and technically little changed from the days of Wellington in the Peninsula fifty years before that. The next major affair to engage the British army was the South African War in the opening years of the century, and this was so different to anything which had gone before that it took some time for the lessons to sink in. But once they had penetrated, it was assumed that a pattern of warfare had developed that would serve as a model for the future. The South African War had been the first major war to involve the use of the high velocity rifle, breech-loading ordnance, smokeless powder, the machine gun, and the open use of country as an integral part of tactics. In the face of the skilful Boer, it was necessary to modify the old-fashioned methods of fighting with artillery. It was no longer practical to deploy guns in a straight line, hub-to-hub, and shoot over open sights at a target some 1,500 to 2,000 yards away, because with a modern rifle the enemy could hide behind a rock and shoot back with perfect impunity and deadly effect. His guns were not so easy to find, because the new powders gave out no clouds of white smoke to reveal his position with every shot. Dun and khaki uniforms rendered troops invisible against the veldt; and the guerilla tactics of the Boers meant that openly disposed guns were liable to sniper attack from any direction. Dispersal became necessary and guns

Oxen-hauled 4.7-inch guns in South Africa foreshadow future problems in moving newer and heavier guns

and their attendant wagons and limbers needed to be concealed in folds of ground, in scrub and bushes, and methods of fire control had to be developed which enabled the guns to be hidden in this fashion and yet their fire controlled so that they did not expose themselves to fire while engaging the enemy.

From all this, and from similar experience undergone by the Japanese and Russian artillery in the Russo-Japanese War at about the same time, the artillerymen of the world sat and discussed the lessons and began to develop fresh tactical ideas. There were, inevitably, numbers of more senior gentlemen who held that the tactics developed in South Africa were an unfortunate aberration peculiar to the time and place, and that the accepted tactics need not be disturbed too much. Because of reactionary caution, much of the proposed modifications were watered down or abandoned altogether, so that while there was a certain amount of interest in the selection of concealed positions and the development of improved methods of fire control, the majority felt that concealment of guns was somehow 'ungentlemanly' and that the greatest tactical feature of artillery was its mobility, its ability to rush into action, fire a few decisive rounds over open sights, and then rapidly depart to repeat the performance at some other point on the battlefield.

Another feature which caused an upheaval in tactical thinking was the recent development of what was then known as the 'Quick-Firing Gun', and this concept demands a little technical exposition in order to show just how important it was.

The last important European war had been the Franco-Prussian War of 1870, and the artillery of that time was such that if one of Edward III's gunners from Crécy of 1346 had been reincarnated and attached to a French or German battery he would soon have felt at home. In the 500 or so years since the invention of the cannon, there had been very little technical advance. The Crimean War was fought with muzzle-loading smooth-bores, and it was not until this was over that the gunmakers of the world began to consider improving the cannon. There had been attempts in the past, it is true, but these had all fallen by the wayside due to the lack of metallurgical and other technical knowledge on the inventor's part. But in the mid-1850s a reasonable amount of technical know-how had been developed, largely due to the Industrial Revolution and the subsequent mechanisation – railways, steam engines, simple machine tools, improved methods of measurement,

With its jaunty sentry, this 4.7-inch naval gun on Captain Percy Scott's extempore field carriage is an inviting target for a sniper, a lesson soon learned on the veldt

the beginnings of mass production and interchangeability. These advances had thrown up a number of ingenious engineers who were now attracted to the military problems of the time, the most intriguing and rewarding of which appeared to be the provision of efficient artillery.

The ironclad ship was the root of the revolution, since more powerful guns were needed to attack such a vessel. Krupp, Erhardt, Armstrong, Schneider, Parrot are names which come readily to the historian's mind when he considers this era, and all of them had something to contribute. First came a method of loading the gun from the breech. This meant that the gunners could remain relatively protected behind cover (either an emplacement or a shield forming part of the gun) while loading, and no longer had to expose themselves to enemy fire while clustering round the muzzle to reload. Three systems became

pre-eminent: the Krupp sliding block, using a brass cartridge case to seal the breech end so that the explosion of the propelling charge was all used up in sending the shell on its way and none leaked out at the back; the Nordenfeldt Eccentric Screw, which also used a cartridge case; and the French De Bange system which used a screw-thread type breech block and a resilient pad to do the sealing. With this latter system the cartridge was simply a cloth bag carrying the charge, since the brass case was now superfluous. There were numerous variations on these systems, but these are the basic three which have stayed the course.

After providing a satisfactory method of loading from the rear end, the next problem to be tackled was the recoil of the gun. The gun of the closing years of the 19th Century was rigidly mounted on its carriage, and when it fired the gun carriage and the gun rolled or jumped back anything from one foot to twenty feet depending on

A typical QF gun of its day, this Krupp 77mm shows the sliding block breech with integral firing mechanism, recoil system carried in a cradle below the barrel, shield, and early Goerz Panoramic sight, which enabled the gunner to aim without seeing his target

its size and the force of the propelling charge. Various methods were adopted to abate this; in wheeled carriages brakes were applied and spades dug into the ground. In fixed guns, such as those in fortresses, heavy carriages were used with ropes to check the recoil movement, or the carriages were arranged to slide up inclined planes. Whatever the system employed, it was merely a palliative, and the gunners had to set to work after the bang and manhandle the gun back to its proper place. It is on record that at the end of the Battle of Waterloo the British gunners were so exhausted that they were unable to manhandle the guns back into position and kept firing them from wherever the recoil had stopped, and by the time the battle was over some of them had recoiled back into the wagon lines and were mixed up with the ammunition limbers and supply carts.

The science of hydraulics was making itself known in industry during the 1850s and 1860s, and it was to hydraulics that the ordnance engineers turned. It seems that one of the Siemens brothers, German-born engineers settled in England, suggested the use of an hydraulic cylinder to the British army in about 1862, and it was soon placed in service in coast gun carriages. The gun carriage had a piston rod attached which pulled a piston through a cylinder filled with a viscous mixture of water and glycerine. Inside the piston was a hole, and the liquid had to pass through the hole to get from one side of the piston to the other as it moved. This flow of liquid acted as a brake, kept the recoil movement damped down and made the gun easier to control. This was merely a brake or buffer though, and did nothing to return the gun to the firing position. Later developments brought in springs to do this job, compressing them on recoil and allowing their expansion to push the gun back.

Translating this idea on to a field gun carriage – which had to be simple, robust, and light enough to be pulled by six horses – was not so easy. Several attempts were made before the problem was solved. The ultimate solution came from France, with their introduction of the 75mm Field Gun, 1897 Model. This was the gun which introduced to a startled military world the principle of axial recoil, and it is the progenitor of all the 'Quick-firing' guns that came after it. The '75' had a simple wheeled carriage which carried a trough-shaped cradle. In this cradle was a cylinder block containing the hydraulic recoil system; the gun slid in guides in the cradle and was attached to a piston rod forming part of the recoil system. It was fitted with a Nordenfeldt breech

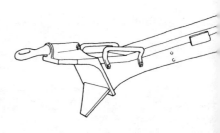

screw and used a 'fixed' round of ammunition, one in which shell and brass cartridge case was attached together like an overgrown rifle cartridge. The gunner threw this round into the breech and closed the block with a 120-degree turn – a simple flick of the wrist to a practised man. The gunlayer took aim and fired. The carriage remained perfectly still, anchored by a small spade at the trail end, but the gun recoiled straight back in its cradle, pulling out the piston rod as it went. It came to a smooth stop after recoiling four feet, then quickly and smoothly slid back into the firing position. On the return stroke, the gunner reached out and flipped the breech open, whereupon the cartridge case was ejected clear of the gun. The next round was loaded

The immortal French 75mm M 1897 field gun, the first modern QF field piece, and the gun upon which the French army relied

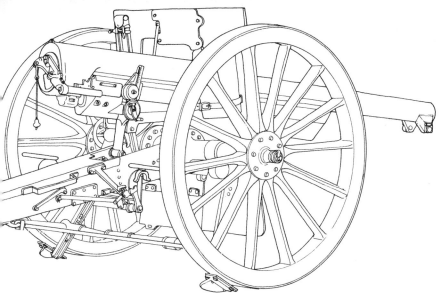

The 75mm field gun, France's most famous artillery piece of the First World War, was still in service in the Second, but with a new carriage more suited to the more sophisticated mechnical transport of the times. Though still a good and reliable weapon, it had by now been completely outclassed by newer guns. *Weight:* 2,700lbs. *Rate of fire:* 6 rounds per minute. *Weight of shell:* 16lbs (shrapnel). *Elevation:* −10 degrees to +19 degrees. *Range:* 7,500 yards

the breech closed, and the gun was ready to fire again.

The principal reason it was ready to fire so quickly was simply that the carriage hadn't moved, the gunners were still kneeling around the gun ready to reload, and the gun layer was still there with his eye near the sight and his hands on the control wheels ready to take aim as soon as the gun was back in place. Because nobody had to leap clear to let the gun recoil, it became worthwhile putting a shield on the gun so as to protect the gunners from rifle or enemy artillery fire while they knelt at work. And so the 'Quick-firing Gun' had arrived; using cased ammunition, preferably fixed, with a rapid-operating breech mechanism, axial recoil on the carriage so that the gun moved but the carriage remained still, and a shield to protect the gunners. This was the gun of the future, and the revelation that the French army actually had such a weapon put the armies of Europe in an uproar.

However, the fact that the French army had the gun was known only by accident. They kept the equipment concealed under wraps, and nobody except the men who actually made it knew what went on inside the recoil system, how it worked, what returned the gun to the firing position, or why it worked so well. No figures for range, rate of fire, shell weight, cartridge weight, or anything else were released, and one or two inquisitive people who tried to find out more about it spent considerable lengths of time inside French prisons for their pains. In an age not noticeably security conscious, this was remarkable. But the French were adamant that nobody was going to know anything about the '75' until they had one pointed at them, by which time it would be too late.

But secrecy breeds rumours, and it wasn't long before military attachés were swapping lies and reporting back quite fantastic claims for what the '75' could do. It could fire sixty rounds

a minute; it had a range of ten miles; the shrapnel shell had bullets of a new alloy which could penetrate anything, and the high explosive shell was so devastating that nothing could possibly stand before it. It was probably the forerunner of all the far-fetched tales about mystery guns with which gunners of all nations have regaled themselves in time of war; it was the precursor of the gun which recoiled so far that they towed the rations up when it ran back, or the one which shot fourteen miles and threw rocks the rest of the way. However much the staffs sought to sift the wheat from the chaff, one thing was obvious any nation which didn't have a quick-firing gun to match the '75' was in a vulnerable state. Parliaments were assailed, home-brewed strategists published pamphlets, and military circles hummed with two basic questions: what sort of gun do we adopt and how do we tailor our tactics to suit? Indeed, reading through some of the arguments which went on around that time, one is irresistably reminded of the uproar in the late 1940s on the advent of the atomic weapon.

The one thing which preyed on every mind was the 'Quick-Firing' (QF label; visions were thrown up of harassed gunners blasting off every round they could lay their hands on as soon as the battle was opened and then being caught without a shot left. A more sober view was that even if discipline prevailed, the ability to fire quickly would undoubtedly be used at times, and what about increasing the ammunition supply? The equation was inevitably made: if X guns could now fire Y shells a minute, where it had needed 3X muzzle-loaders to fire the same amount in years gone by did this mean that the gun strength of the army could be reduced? Would fewer guns capable of firing the same amount of ammunition but quicker effect a better result than the same number of guns firing three times the amount of metal on to the target Nobody thought of the word 'Over

Above: A French 105mm gun at Verdun, 1916. *Below:* Krupp's gun-building shop in 1904. These are naval weapons, but one supposes that equally well-equipped shops were producing field pieces

A Krupp 15cm howitzer with the breech open to show the chamber and rifling. Note the extended cradle which supports the gun during recoil

kill', but the idea was there.

Krupp was quick to produce a similar sort of gun for sale to all comers, and the German army tentatively accepted it as a service weapon. Among its customers was the Japanese army, and the Russo-Japanese War saw the use of QF guns on a large scale for the first time. The British in South Africa had no QFs at all, although they were using breech-loaders with rudimentary systems of recoil control. From these two wars came sufficient information to answer many of the questions. It was now seen that the gunners were too smart to fling their shells in all directions, and the ability to loose off a fast fire at will could be a valuable asset under particular circumstances. Gradually, assumption and fantasy gave way to fact and the QF gun was

assimilated into the world's armies.

Another technical revolution had occurred in the manufacture of the ammunition used with the guns. The old smooth-bores had used cannon-balls; solid for smashing effect against hard targets, and shrapnel for use against men. The introduction of breech-loading rifled ordnance had opened the door to elongated projectiles which could be heavier and have more capacity for a given calibre, but their internal arrangements had to be redesigned and extensively tested before they were acceptable for use. Piercing shot was among the earliest projectiles developed for the new guns, since it will be remembered that the ironclad ship was the target which started the improvements. The shrapnel was redesigned to suit the new guns and became a much more formidable weapon than ever before; the shrapnel shell is nothing more than a flying gun, since inside the projectile are hundreds of lead balls and a small charge of gunpowder. A time fuze at the nose would ignite the powder when the shell was poised over the heads of the enemy troops, and the explosion of the powder would blow out the balls in an expanding cone at high velocity, delivering hundreds of lethal missiles onto the unprotected heads below. In its original cannon-ball form, there was an infinite number of positions the ball could adopt at the moment of bursting, so that the bullets might be fired out in any direction but the right one, but with the rifling of the gun, which kept the nose of the shell pointed to the target throughout its flight, every shrapnel shell fired its deadly contents in the right direction.

Shrapnel was, of course, useless against fortifications or *matériel* and the explosive or 'common' shell was used in that case. This was simply a steel or iron casing with a filling of gunpowder, ignited by an impact fuse. But gunpowder is a 'heaving' explosive, good for blasting or propelling, but poor for the sort of shattering response needed from such a small item as a gun shell.

The years during which the gun had been improved had also seen vast improvements in explosives, with the introduction of such well-known names as dynamite, blasting gelatine, nitroglycerin and picric acid. It was inevitable that the artillerymen would contemplate putting these new and exceptionally powerful substances into shells, but this was easier said than done. All the 'high' explosives are very sensitive: put one in a shell and then fire an explosive charge behind it to send it up a gun barrel and the chances are that the sudden shock will upset the high explosive, there will be a detonation in the bore, and the gun and gunners will be their own victims. Many and varied were the techniques attempted to solve this knotty problem, a common contender being the use of giant air-guns to propel the shells, thus dispensing with the need for a violent blow to get them moving. But the real

answer lay in the development of less sensitive explosives that were still violent in their effect.

Another explosive problem lay in the supersession of gunpowder as the propelling agent. Gunpowder was as old as the gun itself; it had never been improved on as a propelling charge, and its drawbacks were enormous. It was highly sensitive to friction and sparks, and equally sensitive to damp; when the gun fired, it gave out a vast cloud of white smoke which obscured the target and everything around the gun for several minutes, and afterwards the gunners had the task of cleaning out the foul-smelling deposit in the bore which gunpowder always leaves behind it. The discovery of high explosives led to more research into 'low' or propelling explosives, and nitro-cellulose variations were soon being touted as the solution. One of the most common of these was gun-cotton, which was accepted as a propellant in some quarters. Most of these early propellants were serviceable for a short time, and then developed violently unstable characters due to chemical reaction within themselves, largely because of the presence of impurities in the basic materials. When this situation arose magazines would vanish in a cloud of dust without any warning, and eventually many countries completely forbade the manufacture of nitrocellulose explosives until some more basic research had been done.

In due course the chemists succeeded, and Alfred Nobel produced 'Ballistite' followed closely by the British 'Cordite' and the American 'Pyro Powder'. All these were similar in concept, being nitro-cellulose, highly purified, with various admixtures to improve it, make it more powerful, or automatically safeguard it against deterioration. The British 'Cordite', for example, was a mixture of nitro-cellulose and nitro-glycerin, treated with a solvent and extruded in the form of cords – hence the name. Most nations preferred to leave the nitro-glycerin out of the mixtures, since while this produced a much more powerful propellant it also made the flame temperature somewhat above the melting point of steel and wore the gun barrels away at a rapid rate. This was alleviated in the later British Modified Cordite by adding a portion of 'mineral jelly' – commercially famous as 'Vaseline' – which lubricated the gun and also slightly reduced the flame temperature so as to reduce the wear. But above all else, the great advantages of these substances were firstly that they gave more power for their bulk; they were relatively impervious to damp; and they were practically

smokeless when fired – although not without considerable flash.

Finally, after smokeless powders had been introduced, the high explosive shell arrived; after years of trial the British army introduced a shell filled with a substance called 'Lyddite' – commemorating the fact that the testing had been done at the Siege Artillery School at Lydd, in Kent. Although this early attempt at security was praiseworthy, it didn't baffle many people for very long, and it was soon known that Lyddite was simply picric acid which had been melted and cast into the shell, thus becoming somewhat less sensitive to shock than the normal crystalline form. Japan adopted it under the name 'Shimose' and used it against the Russians; Italy called it Pertite, France Melinite, Austria Ecrasite, and America Dunnite. But whatever its name, it still had one fault; the results at the target were often disappointing. The effect was

Loading a German howitzer. Four gunners lift the tray to the breech, from where the shell will be rammed by other men. At the left the gunlayer waits to make the final lay, while on the right another gunner holds the cartridge case with its charge of smokeless powder

contingent upon it being satisfactorily detonated by the shell's fuze, and to do this with one hundred per cent success called for a large detonator of fulminate of mercury. This new negated all the advantages of the new substance because the fulminate detonator was highly sensitive. Some countries were willing to take a chance on it, but none of them liked the idea, and the hunt for a better explosive went on.

Germany turned to trinitrotoluene (TNT) as a better answer, but if anything, it was more difficult to set off satisfactorily than Lyddite had been. But it was also much more stable than picric acid, which had an unpleasant tendency to react chemically with the metal of the shell and form highly nervous compounds which frequently detonated themselves. So the Germans persevered with TNT until they found that the solution to all the problems lay in building a suitably graded train of detonation from the fuse through an 'exploder system' in which the intensity of detonation was gradually amplified until it set off the main explosive filling. Once this system was understood and properly applied, first-order detonations became the rule rather than the exception. Britain followed Germany very closely in the adoption of TNT, and had the same struggle to develop the exploder system, finally solving the problem just before war broke out in 1914.

And having at last arrived at 1914 with some modern ordnance and ammunition, let us see what each of the protagonists owned in the way of artillery, excluding fortress weapons used for coastal defence, since these do not enter our story until later.

During the South African War the British army had been driven to buying a number of QF guns from the German maker, Erhardt, until such time as its own gun designers could come to some decision about what sort of gun the army wanted. These 15-pounders were not as robust as the army would have liked, but they were sound enough and provided the gunners with vitally needed experience in the handling of a modern gun. As a result of the South African War, a committee had been formed to examine the requirements of horse and field artillery and report thereon, and the result of this report was the development of two weapons, the 13-pounder and the 18-pounder. The former was a 3-inch gun firing a 12½lb shrapnel shell containing 263 bullets at a velocity of 1,658 feet per second, while the latter was a 3.3-inch, with an 18½lb shrapnel shell holding 364 bullets and firing at 1,590 feet per second. Arguments waxed loud and long as to which should be adopted. In the end, to break the impasse, a unique solution was devised. The problem was taken to the Prime Minister – non-army, non-artillery, strictly disinterested – and dropped into his unwilling lap. His answer was true to the spirit of British compromise – have some of both. So the Horse Artillery, more mobile since their task was to support the faster-moving cavalry, were equipped with the 13-pounder, while the slower-moving Field Artillery took the 18-pounder. In the event, this apparently compromise decision turned out to be the right one. Both equipments served their allotted tasks well, though by the nature of the war itself, the 18-pounder became the more numerous.

In addition to these field guns, the British army had realised, by its experience in South Africa, that a howitzer firing a heavier shell was a useful adjunct to a field army for dropping shells behind ridges and hills where the flat-trajectory guns could not reach. At the same time as the Field Gun Committee had deliberated, another committee had gone to work on howitzer specifications and had circulated its requirements to various gunmakers. Numerous contesting designs were tried, the winner being a 4.5-inch design from the Coventry Ordnance Works, which was im-

Above : The British 13-pounder Horse Artillery gun, together with its ammunition limber. *Below :* The original model British 18-pounder became the standard gun throughout the Empire

Below : In 1918 the greatly-improved 18-pounder Mark 4 appeared. The box trail allowed greater elevation, the extended cradle made the gun much steadier, the hydro-pneumatic recoil system was more efficient and reliable, and the improved sights made the gun more accurate

mediately adopted.

The field guns and howitzers were light and suited for horse draught in a condition ready for speedy action. Heavier metal was supplied by a variety of guns and howitzers which were rather less mobile and often required assembly or long preparation before opening fire. Again, the South African War had shown the necessity for these cannon. There was, for example, a 4.7-inch gun which had been the brainchild of Captain Percy Scott, one of the Royal Navy's foremost gunnery experts. Seeing that heavy support was lacking on the South African battlefields, he simply had some high-velocity 4.7-inch guns dismounted from a convenient warship, got the local railway shops to construct some Rube Goldberg carriages, and had them oxen-hauled to the scene of battle to give the soldiers a hand. Manned by straw-hatted sailors, they provided some very welcome long-range cover, and no doubt added a certain amount of colour to the battlefield. Benefiting from Scott's lesson, proper carriages were designed for 4.7-inch guns provided in more regular fashion to go on them, and the 4.7 joined the army officially. A 5-inch howitzer was also in the 'siege train', as were a 6-inch gun and a 6-inch howitzer, though these were in small numbers and more in the nature of extended trials. Finally a 9.2-inch howitzer supplied by the Coventry Ordnance Works was undergoing trials at the Siege Artillery range near Rhyader in the Welsh mountains during the summer of 1914, though most people believed that there would be few opportunities to deploy such a monster in modern war, unless a full-scale siege developed.

France, of course, swore by its faithful 75mm Model 1897. This fired a 16lb shell filled with 300 bullets and also had a high explosive shell filled with Melinite. But what France lacked was a howitzer for the field units. One had been designed, but during trials it had shot so badly that the trials had been abandoned and the designers sent back to start again. While the designers designed, the Chamber of Deputies argued the cost of providing the army with howitzers, and eventually one member, Malandrin, proposed a solution which seemed to the politicians to be admirable. His system was simply to fit a flat disc around the nose of the 75mm gun shell. This would spoil the ballistic shape so that the trajectory would no longer be flat, but would rapidly adopt a steep angle of descent due to air drag. Given that the gunners would now have to use a higher elevation to attain the same range, it meant that with the Malandrin Disc added, the shell would point down more sharply over the target, and *voilà!* a howitzer. The gunners were not convinced, but then they did not control the pursestrings; so instead of field howitzers, which they badly needed, they were given boxes of Malandrin Discs on two different sizes and told to 'shut up and get on with it'.

However, some expenditure had got past the alert guardians of the public purse. By 1914 an order had been given for eighty 75mm horse artillery guns to be made by Schneider, to be delivered in time for the autumn manoeuvres; this was to fire the same shell as the field gun, but with a less powerful charge so that the gun would be lighter, as befitted a horse artillery piece. Also 200 120mm guns were to be delivered by December 1915, and 120 of the older 120mm guns were to be converted to the latest specification by the same date. Finally a mountain gun, the 2.65-inch Ducrest, had been issued in 1912. This was a remarkable weapon, using the differential or dynamic recoil system – a system which had a number of promoters at that time. The object was to damp out gun recoil with as little weight as possible, and so it was a firm contender for consideration in mountain equipments, since these had to be dismantled and carried on mule-back. The method of controlling recoil was

Above : The 4.7-inch gun was also improved by making a better carriage, and it became a standard medium gun. *Below :* The elderly British 5-inch howitzer still had a place in France in 1915, but it was soon to be replaced by the 6-inch versions

Below : The 6-inch 26cwt howitzer, which gradually replaced all the earlier 5-inch and 6-inch models, remained in service until the 1940s. The 'traction-engine wheels' were supplemented by hinged pattens in order to give greater flotation over mud

Above : At the beginning of the war many elderly French guns were called into service. This 120mm, seen in the Argonne in 1914, has no recoil system, rudimentary sights and the breech mechanism is of the obsolete and slow-acting ring carrier type. The trunnions on the trail body are to hold the gun while travelling. *Below :* The German 77mm M 1906, captured at Serches in 1914. Like most of its contemporaries, the elevation, and thus range, are limited by the trail construction

to haul the gun back against a powerful spring, or compressed air, until it was locked back in what, in any other gun, would be considered the fully recoiled position. It was then loaded. On tripping a lever, the gun was released and flew forward under the spring or air pressure until it reached the forward position. Fractionally before it arrived, it fired, and thus the explosion force had first to arrest the forward-moving mass of the gun and then reverse its motion and make it recoil. Consequently, the recoil mechanism could be simple and light, since most of the work was done in arresting the forward movement of the gun. Once it had recoiled fully, it was caught and held there ready for the next shot. The only real drawback was that if the cartridge missed fire, the gun was liable to slam over on to its nose, but the whole system demanded a nice adjustment of spring pressures and propelling charge, and it failed to make many converts.

French heavy artillery was provided in small numbers with 155mm Rimailho howitzers on a scale of four per army corps, and six short 155mm howitzers per army corps as medium artillery. This disproportion was due to the French conviction that a large number of light guns – 75s – could swamp a target with fire and hence render heavy guns superfluous. Here was the QF theory gone mad.

The principal German field artillery gun was the 77mm Model of 1906, firing a 15lb shell containing 300 bullets at 1,525 feet per second. A high explosive shell was also provided, but Germany pinned its faith on the Krupp Universal' shell. This was a cross between high explosive and shrapnel, achieved in one of two ways. Either the head of the shell was made as a separate unit carrying a charge of TNT, or the lead bullets in the shrapnel section were packed in a matrix of TNT. In the former pattern, the time fuze could be set to operate in the air in the usual way in which case the bullets were blown out as missiles and

the explosive head was projected forward as a separate missile, landing roughly in the middle of the shrapnel's impact area and detonating on arrival. If the fuze was set to operate on impact, then the detonation of the head unit would damage *matériel* and the shrapnel would be blown about the place for missile effect. In the second design, a time fuze would discharge the bullets in the normal way while impact functioning would detonate the TNT to give the same double effect on both men and *matériel*. Like most multi-purpose designs, it was a compromise, being neither so good a shrapnel shell as a pure shrapnel design, nor so good a high explosive shell as one filled solely with explosive. But it was quite effective, and, fired in quantity by QF guns, was a devastating missile.

Germany had also seen the need for howitzers – having studied the South African War from afar – and was provided with a 105mm light field howitzer firing a 281lb shell at 1,083 feet per second. This was backed up by a number of 15cm howitzers with 871lb shells. At the top of the tree, and held in conditions of great secrecy, was the Krupp-built 42cm howitzer, bigger than any gun ever envisaged by any other nation as a field weapon, and owing its presence to Germany's continental location. Surrounded principally by land frontiers which were strongly fortified, any move by the German army was bound to be checked sooner or later by concrete and armour plate. So in order to deal with this type of target when the need arose, the enormous 42cm 'mortars' were secretly commissioned, built and tested, and then stored away. Their day was soon to come.

Russia was as great a mystery in 1914 as she was in 1941, and her habit of buying guns from abroad, altering the designs to suit her own convenience and producing them in her own arsenals, away from prying eyes, left the Intelligence staffs of the west the difficult task of trying to decide

Above : The German 105mm howitzer M98/09 in action. Presumably posed, as pipe-smoking in action is not usually encouraged. *Below :* The Russian 76.2mm field gun 1903 with a businesslike crew

what she did and did not have. The 1900 Model field gun, still in service in quantity, was a relic of the Russo-Japanese War, and was one of the few weapons which ever went to war with ndia-rubber as the prime mover in the recoil system. The gun was mounted on a top carriage which could slide along the top of the trail assembly. nside the trail, running right down he length, were india-rubber 'dough-nuts' which were compressed by the recoil and which pushed the gun back nto battery afterwards. The system worked – just – but it was not wildly uccessful; moreover the sights, being ixed to the top carriage, recoiled with he gun, which produced very alert nd agile gunlayers but no other noticeable advantages; the gun was ar too heavy; and it had no shield. Designed by General Engelhardt and uilt in the Tsar's Putilov Arsenal, it red a 15lb shell at the high velocity of ,950 feet per second. Such perfor-nance was too good to lose: it was thus ecided to redesign the carriage to do way with the drawbacks but keep the un as it was. By 1903 a hydraulic uffer had been designed with springs o return the gun to battery, a shield was fitted, and the sights relocated on non-recoiling part of the weapon.

In the howitzer field, several con-enders were trying to make their hareholders happy by landing a nice t contract. Krupp supplied a number f 120mm weapons, which it hoped to cense for production at Putilov. A chneider 155mm design had been ubmitted for trial, while a number of 5mm long range guns and 15cm owitzers of doubtful antecedents were eld by the heavy artillery brigades. The Austro-Hungarian Empire's rtillery was in the throes of re-ganisation. The field gun was a 77mm ring a 15lb shrapnel with 332 bullets ; 1,640 feet per second, but the owitzer field was wide open. An old ttern of 105mm was still in use, a esign relying on a spring spade to eck the recoil. This system, which d been tried by most countries in

the 1890s, involved connecting a robust spade to the gun carriage by a spring of some sort, then digging the spade in and allowing the whole gun and car-riage to recoil over it and then be forced back by the spring action.

Probably the best method of using this system was the design in which the spade was suspended from the carriage axle and attached to the trail by a steel rope to a spring. When the gun moved back, the point of the spade would dig in more and more and the gun would pivot back across it, pulling on the rope and compressing the spring. When recoil stopped, the spring would pull back on the rope and thus heave the carriage back over the spade. One advantage of this system was that the spade was never dug in except while the gun was actually recoiling, so that changes in direction would be easier to make, without having to dig the whole spade out of the ground. Differential recoil had been tried and abandoned, and an Erhardt design had been finally ap-proved for issue, after an abortive attempt to convert the spring-spade model to long recoil.

The Erhardt design was interesting, since it was one of the first guns to use controlled variable recoil. In a howit-zer, most of the firing is done at high angles of elevation. Consequently, if the gun is slung about its point of balance – common practice then with field guns – the breech will strike the ground at full recoil and high angle unless the gun is set very high off the ground. If the recoil stroke is made short in order to avoid this, it then becomes violent when the gun is fired horizontally, because at horizontal the energy tries to move back and lift the gun wheels from the ground, whereas at high elevation the recoil force is more downward and tends to anchor the equipment more securely to the ground. In order to get over this anomaly, the variable recoil system permits a long recoil stroke when the gun is horizontal, but as the gun is elevated a gear device alters the orifices in the hydraulic buffer, so as to choke down the recoil stroke to a shorter length. In the Austrian Erhardt howitzer the recoil at horizontal was fifty-six inches, but only thirty-two inches when the gun was fully elevated to fifty-five degrees.

The Austrian heavy howitzer was an elderly 15cm without any provision for recoil at all, and this was scheduled to be replaced some time in 1915 with a more modern design. But the greatest strength of the Austro-Hungarian artillery was the force of super-heavy Skoda howitzers of 21 and 30.5cm calibre. The 21cm was known slightly abroad, but the 30.5cm was entirely concealed, except for a few rumours and wild guesses which were discounted by sober judges.

The remaining countries of Europe were largely equipped by Krupp, Erhardt or Schneider from their stock models, and their weapons differed little from the pattern outlined above. The artillery strength of Turkey had been augmented during 1913 in an unusual way; she had intercepted a shipment of Schneider 75mm field guns *en route* to Serbia, and fifty-two of these were inducted into service.

One final point about the artillery of 1914 needs to be mentioned, and that is the question of how the guns were going to be brought into action when the time came. A single British field battery required 168 horses to move it to war. During peacetime this number was reduced to seventy, but on mobilisation the missing ninety-eight had to be provided quickly. To cope with this the Army Horse Reserve had been established shortly before the war. The artillery section of this reserve had 10,000 horses marked down and on call at forty-eight hours notice; for this the owners were paid a retainer of £4 a year, and their horses were inspected every six months. Originally there was to be no payment, merely a reliance on patriotic spirit, but at the behest of various trade organisations the payment was introduced. For, as it was

pointed out, £4 per year per horse to a tradesman could mean the difference between the horse making a profit and making a loss; and if the horse made a loss, the trader might well exchange it for a motor lorry. The appeal seems to have worked, for when the balloon went up the horses were all delivered to their mobilisation depôts within a specified time.

Germany had a more sophisticated system. A census of motor vehicles held there in 1913 shows the surprising figures of 7,700 heavy trucks and 50,000 automobiles in use. The heavy truck number is interesting, because the German army operated a scheme whereby if a businessman purchased a truck, the army would pay $35 towards the purchase price and $15 a year thereafter for five years, the reserve the use of the truck on mobilisation. After five years the owner was relieved of his obligation, $1,100 to the good, but if during the five years mobilisation was called, he lost the truck. By this means, the army had

bove : This German 77mm gun, M 1916, shows the increased elevation achieved by
dopting a box trail and trunnioning the gun at the rear. *Below :* An Austrian M 1915
ountain gun in position in a forward area on the Somme

Turkish artillery in action with their Krupp-built 75mm gun. The open deployment and cluster of binocular-flourishers close to the gun is typical of prewar tactics, to be severely changed within a few months

built up a reserve of 1,500 trucks by 1914. Just how many of these were earmarked for artillery is not known, though it is known that no trucks were used for towing guns.

Most nations had made some experiments with motor traction before the war. Italy had placed a Fiat truck – or motor-limber, as it was known then – in service as early as 1911, towing their Krupp 15cm howitzer. Austria showed two 24cm howitzers being truck-towed in pieces on their 1912 manoeuvres, and in the same year the French had fielded a battery of 12cm siege guns, one of 21cm siege guns, and one 24cm howitzer all truck-drawn. But to show just what could be done in mobility, the British army

The Skoda 30.5cm howitzer, an ace up the sleeve of the Austro-Hungarian army

indulged in a spectacular display in July 1914 when the West Riding of Yorkshire Territorial Artillery roared into action against an imaginary enemy, towing their Erhardt 15-pounders behind four 30hp Sheffield-Simplex touring cars. Guns and limbers bowled along behind while the gunners rode in comfort in the tonneau, and the battery made an average speed of twenty-one miles per hour over a 120-mile manoeuvre. It was splashed in the popular newspapers, but it didn't worry the Army Horse Reserve very much.

The opening shots

When the armies moved in August 1914, their artillery components were roughly on a par. Each French army corps had thirty 4-gun batteries of 75mm guns and six short-barrel 155mm howitzers. The German corps held eighteen 6-gun batteries of 77mm guns and six of 105mm howitzers, with sixteen heavy howitzers in support, so although weaker in field guns it was considerably stronger in howitzers. The British corps contained eighteen 6-gun batteries of 18-pounders and six of 4.5-inch howitzers, plus two four-gun batteries of 60-pounders. The actual number of barrels per corps was thus – British 154, French 126 and German 160. Not only were the French deficient in barrels, but they had pinned far too much faith on the quick-firing concept, and were convinced that the storm of fire from a well-handled battery of 75s was sufficient to counterbalance the heavier shells but slower rate of fire to be got from howitzers. How much of this was

honest belief and how much was rationalisation in the face of a government who refused to finance the production of howitzers is hard to say, but certainly this reliance on rate of fire was in line with the '*l'audace, toujours l'audace*' philosophy which ran through the French army at the time. But almost the first action of the war revealed the power of the howitzer at its most damaging and effective.

The German plan of advance envisaged a wide sweeping envelopment through Belgium against the Allied left flank. This unexpected move would, it was firmly believed, so dislocate the Allies that a follow-up thrust by Germany against the French in the central front could not fail to succeed. This move was duly started, and by the afternoon of 4th August the German army was outside Liège.

The Belgians, in years gone by, had insured against just such a German move by fortifying the whole Liège area with an encircling belt of twelve forts, constructed to the designs of one of the nineteenth century's most brilliant military engineers, H A Brialmont. The forts were built during the years 1888-91, completely outdating all other fortifications and forming the pattern to be followed by those erected in other countries in later years. Instead of adopting the old idea of a continuous curtain wall around the town, Brialmont moved the forts out and made each completely detached from its companions. It was suggested that the gaps between the forts should be filled with outworks and entrenchments which could be manned by support troops when the occasion arose, but Brialmont was entirely against this modification. The forts were sited carefully so as to cover every approach to Liège and also to cover each other with fire – on

Daily maintenance on a British 4.5-inch howitzer, 1914. The gun is depressed for checking the recoil system and the breech block has been removed for cleaning

the map. Unfortunately the ground was not quite as forgiving as the maps were, and some forts found they had a fair amount of dead ground in their areas. Extra redoubts and outworks could have covered these, but the twelve forts were considered so invulnerable that further outworks were believed unnecessary.

The forts themselves were of massive construction, an immense thickness of concrete, largely concealed beneath the surface of the ground but with concrete keeps protruding from the centre of their triangular ground plan. The 'trace' or boundary of the fort was a deep and broad ditch of a new design; the 'approved' ditch of previous forts was vertically sided, with both the sides of stone or concrete and water at the bottom. The inner face would be loopholed, and periodically a *caponière* or covered passage would run across the ditch. These *caponières* were pierced on each side with loopholes for rifles or for cannon loaded with case-shot, and were for sweeping the ditch to repel attackers.

Brialmont's ditch was vertically walled on the outer side only, and this wall was loopholed for rifles and machine guns sited so as to take an attacking enemy in the rear while attempting to cross the ditch. Instead of water, the bottom was covered with a mass of barbed wire, partly concealed by the grass and undergrowth which grew up among it. The inner wall of the ditch, or 'scarp', was no more than a grassy bank, completely without defensive works. But if an attacker survived the ditch and scaled the grassy slope of the scarp, he was then open to the fire of the defenders in the keep and the other outworks within the fort itself. To defend the keep Brialmont employed his favourite device—turretted guns. The turret mount for land fortifications was a purely continental development which had been pioneered by the German ironmaster, Gruson, in the 1870s. He perfected a technique of

Above : French 155mm howitzer ; these were to form the backbone of the US and French artillery for many years to come. *Below :* German 77mm M 96 after being captured by Australians. This has an extension sight bracket to allow the sight to be used without folding the top of the shield

casting armour plate in a hemispherical shape and, with a gun inside, showing only its muzzle, these were taken up avidly by the contemporary fortress engineers. Basically they were like battleship turrets, metal columns carried deep in concrete, with ammunition hoists and stairs inside to supply the turret and gun at the top. With the lower edge of the hemisphere shielded by an armour belt, the turret offered a small target and one which presented a curved face to the attacking projectile at any angle. Hence even a direct hit was more likely to ricochet than to penetrate. Gruson's turrets had withstood many and varied punishing tests by fire, in trial ranges, and were an accepted defence measure of the age. Below the keep and the turrets lay a complex of accommodation, stores, offices, water cisterns and magazines, all protected by concrete. By all accounts, Brialmont's structural genius deserted him when it came to more pedestrian matters, and the accom-

German 105mm gun abandoned to advancing US troops

modation left a great deal to be desired. It is recorded, for example, that one fort's latrines were situated inside the counterscarp of the ditch at the rear of the fort, which meant a long stroll down a dark tunnel whenever nature called.

Had these forts been suitably built and armed, they might have survived. But they carried within themselves the seeds of their destruction. In the first place, when Brialmont designed the forts in 1888, he had little idea of what power future artillery might achieve. He fell into the same trap that awaited the designers of tanks in the 1930s in making his defence good enough to resist his own attacking weapons, without giving too much thought to what sort of weapons somebody else might produce. His preferred weapon for attack was the 21cm gun, so he designed his concrete to withstand

35

Fort Loncin after the bombardment:
mute testimony to the power of the
concrete-piercing shells

attack from this calibre. His other weakness was under-gunning the fortresses; no more than eight heavy guns, of which two might be 21cm and the remainder 12 or 15cm, were in each fort for major defence, backed by a scattering of 75mm guns for local defence of the immediate surroundings. This dearth of guns meant that the whole 'area of influence' of the fort could never be properly covered; with the two 21cm guns engaged on a target, crucial action could be developing elsewhere, out of range of the smaller weapons. This is not only a matter of design; it is compounded by the inevitable question 'If we give you more guns, where are you going to find the soldiers to man them?' Guns have to be fired by somebody, and forts bristling with artillery, with walls liberally loopholed for rifles and machine guns, can ab-

sorb as many men as an infantry brigade without blinking an eye. So between the shortage of guns and the shortage of men, the Liège forts finished up undergunned, undermanned, but nonetheless formidable.

The German army, however, was not dismayed by the prospect of attacking the forts. It was quite convinced that it could roll forward and 'bounce' the forts. Consequently it tore forwards, filtered between the forts in the dead ground under covering fire from field artillery, and stormed against the first forts with a simple infantry attack. This was a mistake. The garrisons may not have been particularly efficient, but fortifications do give an advantage, and the attacks were contemptuously beaten off and the German advance halted. The town of Liège was captured by the infiltration tactic which took the Germans past the line of forts; but so long as the forts remained inviolate further advance was impossible, since the forts commanded the river crossings which were the only ones in the line of advance. It was time to bring in the howitzers.

The howitzers were 42cm calibre (16.5-inch) weapons which had been developed by Krupp over a period of years. Krupp's had always been keen researchers in the field of large steel castings, every industrial exhibition of the 1890s and 1900s having at least one monster casting on show, each bigger than the last. It was all good fun and kept the competition on its toes. But having cast a bigger lump of steel than anyone else, one might be at a loss what to do with it after the Gold Medals have been collected and the exhibition closed. Not Krupp. He took his lumps home, bored a hole in them and began experimenting with bigger and better guns. By 1900 he had developed a 30.5cm (12-inch) coast mortar firing an 800lb shell to 10,000 yards. This was the successor to a 240mm model, and

in order to keep the development secret, code names were adopted, the 240mm being 'Alpha' and the 30.5cm 'Beta'. 'Beta' went through one or two modifications, and by about 1908 it was decided to build something heavier, with the express purpose of defeating the strongest concrete fortifications liable to be encountered. This was to be 'Gamma', and a calibre of 42cm and a 2,100lb shell was set as the target. Professor Rausenberger, one of Krupp's most brilliant designers, got to work on the gun and the ballistic calculations regarding shell weight and shape, rifling and powder charge needed were done by Captain Becker, the famous ballistician. By 1911 proof firings were done, and it was found that 'Gamma' was phenomenally accurate and ranged to about 16,000 yards. The

The German 42cm 'Bertha' howitzer loaded and ready to fire

design of suitable shells gave some trouble; the original shells carried 140 kilogrammes of TNT poured in from the base. The shells were pointed and fuzed in the base so as to smash through stone, concrete or earthwork protection, pass into the fort and then detonate. Some peculiar results during trials against concrete led to the discovery that the TNT was not adhering to the walls or base of the shell on impact with the concrete, due to cavities formed in the explosive when it cooled. This was cured by pre-pressing the TNT into shaped blocks and anchoring them inside the shell with special shock-resisting cement. A variety of shells of different weights and shapes were tested in order to determine the optimum combination for best ballistic performance coupled with maximum penetrative performance, and a 1,150-kilogramme shell was finally standardised.

As originally conceived, 'Gamma' was to be transported piecemeal by rail and assembled at the required site, since there appeared to be no other way of moving such a large piece of ordnance, the whole weapon weighing 175 tons. However the German army demanded that it be made road-mobile, and since the weight was against such a solution, a redesign was started. This became 'Gamma M' or the 42cm Morser L/14, and was ready in 1913. Lightening the weapon and shortening the bore by two calibres had reduced the maximum range to 10,250 yards. But the whole thing was now transportable in five loads towed by Daimler Benz tractors. No 1 wagon was the 'Appliance Wagon' which carried the hoist used for assembly, ground anchors, tackle, ropes and blocks, and some small carriage components such as elevating and traversing gears, loading crane, trays and so forth. No 2 wagon was the platform wagon, carrying a U-shaped steel frame. No 3 wagon carried the cradle of the howitzer and the special recoil spade. No 4 was the carriage, the rear wheels being the

carriage wheels attached to the trail with a pair of front wheels attached for towing and removed when emplaced. Finally the No 5 wagon carried the barrel and breech mechanism. The battery comprised two such trains, attended by 200 gunners and eighty drivers and mechanics, and it was KMK 3 (Kurz Marin Kanone Battery No 3) which now moved down the dusty August road to Liège.

The first requirement when intending to fire a gun weighing 42$\frac{1}{4}$ tons is to make sure the emplacement can take the weight and shock. Several stories have been told to the effect that suitable sites for the bombardment of the Liège Forts had been purchased in prewar days by truck farmers of German or pro-German antecedents. It was said that they had constructed henhouses, hay barns and what you will all with immensely thick concrete floors; when the time came these structures were knocked down, and lo and behold, the floors were platforms for the 42cm howitzers, correctly shaped and aligned on their targets. It's a familiar story. I've heard it told about garages in Singapore, shanties in Hong Kong, barns outside Leningrad, farmhouses outside Port Arthur – in fact wherever a siege howitzer has been deployed. Needless to say, there is never any truth in it. Had such foundations been available at Liège, one assumes KMK 3 would have been quicker in arriving and the abortive infantry assaults would never have taken place. In any case, heavy concrete foundations, while very acceptable if time allowed, were unnecessary. Any flat piece of ground would do, and if it were not sufficiently firm, a reinforcing fill of stone or a lattice-work of steel girders was easily laid. Indeed, one position selected later in the action was a paved square in Liege itself.

Once the position had been selected, the gun train moved in. No 1 wagon was rapidly unloaded and the four-legged hoist erected over the platform site. The tractor was located just ahead, and a winch cable run back. No 2 wagon was then brought up, attached to the cable, and hauled into place under the hoist. The gun platform was lifted from the wagon and the wagon dragged away, and the platform lowered onto the site, levelled and oriented into the line of fire. No 3 wagon was then hauled on to the platform, the recoil spade hoisted off and laid to one side, and the cradle hoisted up and suspended. No 3 wagon was then pulled away and No 4 brought in, under the hanging cradle; the trail unit and wheels were centred on the platform and secured, the transport wheels removed, and then the cradle lowered into place in the trunnions of the carriage. To complete the assembly, No 5 wagon was then winched up the platform to a point where the barrel could be slid from its transporter into the carriage cradle and bolted to the recoil system. Finally, the spade was hoisted up and placed in position and the traversing, elevating and loading apparatus fitted.

The spade was an enormous steel casting which not only helped to check recoil but also carried a toothed arc which, engaged by a traverse gear train on the carriage, allowed the whole impressive mass to be easily pivoted on the platform to allow accurate pointing over a large arc.

The shell fired by 'Gamma M' was of 820 kilogrammes (1,800lbs) and was propelled by a 50-kilogramme charge. While 10,250 yards was the maximum possible range, the greatest accuracy was achieved at about 9,500 yards, and most of the firing was done at this, or a lesser, range.

These weapons had not been disclosed in prewar days, and when they were eventually announced – at their Liège debut – their details were carefully concealed from the Press. But what reporters could not find out they invented, and with these additions and some local colour thrown in, some wonderful tales abounded and have become articles of faith ever since. One such tale was that the howitzers were manned entirely by Krupp engineers who, sensible of their position,

The Skoda factory at Pilsen in 1917

Gustav (at the wheel) and Bertha Krupp von Bohlen und Halbach in 1913. Bertha's namesakes appeared on the battlefield in the following year, but Gustav had to wait until 1942 before he was honoured in a similar way

took care to don morning suits and top hats before opening fire. Actually, this tale had its origin in the fact that a number of Krupp workers and engineers were officers and NCOs in the Artillery Reserve, and, on being mobilised, they were sent to KMK 3 where their particular talents were of obvious value; a rare military instance of round pegs fitted neatly into round holes.

At half past six on the evening of 12th August all was ready. Observers were posted, in telephonic communication with the guns; command post staffs had calculated bearing and range to the targets, the guns had been oriented, the ammunition unpacked. By each howitzer the gunners were at their posts and the order to load was

given. The barrels were dropped to the horizontal and the breech handles cranked to roll the huge sliding blocks clear of the chambers. The first shells were rolled down a plank path and heaved into the tray hanging from the loading crane. With six men on the crank handles the shell was hoisted into the air and then swung until the tray was positioned in the breech. Now half a dozen men picked up the rammer and positioned it behind the shell; from the rammer staff, knotted ropes were thrown forward to another dozen men alongside the platform. With a rush and a heave, the shell was rammed home, the rotating band wedging into the rifling with that clear bell-like ring which indicates that the shell has been soundly rammed home. The 18-inch brass cartridge case with its load of smokeless powder was then hoisted up and slid into the breech, and finally the handle twirled to slide the block back and lock it in place. The howitzer was then elevated, the firing lanyard hooked up and all was ready.

Another piece of folklore surrounding these weapons is that when they were about to fire everybody in the area lay flat on the ground, and the firing was done electrically from a pit 200 yards away. This tale was circulated in order to overawe the layman with an image of the immense power of the gun, but as any practising gunner will tell you, the bigger the gun, the less the noise. The 42cm was fired by a soldier standing on the platform, pulling a four-foot lanyard to snap a firing pin against a percussion cap in the cartridge case.

And at twenty minutes to seven on that August evening, some unsung German *Kanonier* did just that, and the first 1800lb shell was on its was to Fort Pontisse on a trajectory three miles high, and taking a full minute to get to its target. The crash of the bursting shell, falling some distance from the fort, convinced every Belgian within earshot that the fort's magazine had detonated; nothing else could possibly have made such a noise. The defenders of Pontisse, on the other hand, seeing the fountain of earth and flame erupt, came to the conclusion that an attempt at mining – the age-old classic formula for breaching a fort by tunnelling beneath the wall and blowing it – had come to a premature conclusion. But when a second and a third explosion followed, creeping closer to the fort each time, it eventually dawned on them that they were being subjected to something new and fearsome in the artillery line.

The eighth shell landed squarely on top of the Fort Pontisse keep, penetrating the concrete roof as if it were cheese, and causing death and desolation inside. Having found the range, KMK then closed down and went to bed, leaving the garrison in the fort to clean up the wreckage and worry about the next day; a masterly stroke of psychological warfare.

The next day brought ruin and destruction; the second howitzer of the battery, having been supplied with the data from the previous night's shooting, now joined in. Shell after shell ripped into the fort, peeling armour plate away like cardboard and shattering concrete to dust, blowing cupolas, turrets, guns and gunners high into the air, and burying the garrison under layers of rubble. Survivors' reports speak of terrible conditions within the tunnels and casements; fumes, dust, the stench of excrement – for the ill-sited latrines had been isolated – conditions unheard of before and insupportable to the garrison. By 1230 hours they had had enough; a white flag was hoisted on the rubble and the fort surrendered.

The battery immediately switched to data calculated for Fort Embourg and continued their battering without a pause, to the same effect. Embourg surrendered at 1730 hours. The remainder of the day was spent in firing a few ranging rounds at Fort Liers from one howitzer and at Fort Fleron from the other. Then firing stopped for the day, and the gunners, after preparing ammunition for the next day, took a well-earned rest.

From then on the story of the Liège forts is one of repetition. The howitzers opened fire on each fort in turn; the defenders stood it as long as they could, then surrendered; and the howitzers turned to the next fort. In this way all the forts to the east of the town were subdued, and the 'Big Berthas' as the gunners had now christened their charges, were pulled out of action and moved into the town of Liège in order to take on the remaining western forts, Flematte, Hollogne and Loncin, the last of which was the HQ of General Leman, commanding the defence. After only nineteen shells had landed, the defence of Loncin came to an abrupt end when a shell penetrated the magazine and detonated its entire contents, opening up the fort like a volcano. Among the wreckage, the Germans found General Leman semi-conscious, and the guiding hand of the defence was made a prisoner. Seeing the violent end of

Above : An old pattern German 15cm howitzer. With no recoil system and a short trail, these were unstable weapons when fired. *Below :* They were soon superseded by this vastly improved model. *Below right :* The Austro-Hungarian 24cm howitzer during peacetime practice firing

Fort Loncin, and doubtless fearful of the consequences should they receive a similar shot, the two other forts surrendered, and on 16th August the story of Liège was over.

For the Allies, General Leman's dogged defence had at least bought them time for the French armies to organise themselves. So far as the Germans were concerned, it had confirmed their wisdom in building the 42cm howitzers. They had originally considered that it might take as much as fourteen days battering to crack Liège if the initial 'bounce' failed – as it did; but thanks to 'Big Bertha' it was all over in four days. The Germans then correctly assessed that more fortifications would have to be met, and more howitzers provided.

But if the provision of additional howitzers was desirable, it was not an immediate possibility. The two Berthas of KMK 3 were the only two in existence, and the one and only 'Gamma' was far too cumbersome to rail up and then drag across country.

However, it was at this point that another of the great Continental gunmakers – Skoda, cannon-builder extraordinary to the Austro-Hungarian army – stepped into the breach.

Skoda had considerable experience of producing heavy howitzers, primarily for coast defence; but in the early 1900s he had begun developing road-mobile weapons, beginning with the 24cm 'Gretel' and then going on to build a 30.5cm model which was tested extensively at the Steinfeld experimental range near Wiener Neustadt during 1911 and 1912, and issued to the Austrian army in 1913. It was basically 'Gretel' enlarged; there was a platform or 'bed' which was buried in the ground, a carriage body pivoting on this bed, a cradle with hydro-pneumatic recoil gear, and the barrel. This varied according to the model, the original pattern (Model 11) being 10 calibres long, and the improved version (Model 14) 14 calibres long, a change which boosted the range from 9,600 to 12,000 metres.

Austrian 30.5cm howitzer. A unit of the road train of 'Schlanke Emma', the Skoda 30.5cm howitzer. The Austro-Daimler tractor is towing a carriage and a howitzer barrel

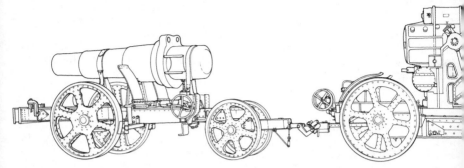

A battery of these consisted of two howitzers, and each was transported by three wagons, one carrying the barrel, one the platform, and one made up by attaching wheels to the carriage body. Each load weighed about ten tons, and 120hp Austro-Daimler tractors were provided for towing, though not, as might be expected, one per trailer. Instead the weapons travelled always as a battery, with one tractor towing a barrel and carriage, the second towing the same components for the second gun, and the third tractor towing two platform wagons. On good flat roads, one tractor was quite capable of pulling one complete howitzer in its three loads, a total of twenty-nine tons, but the other system was preferred since it gave each tractor a load of about twenty tons. After these loads, came another tractor with three wagons, carrying loading cranes, tools, and miscellaneous stores for both howitzers, and then another three-wagon train with the observation parties and their fire control equipment. Finally came thirteen motor trucks with ammunition, one with rations, and a workshop truck, all of which must have made an impressive sight as it rumbled past at its regulation twenty-two kilometres per hour.

The process of coming into action was much the same with 'Schlanke Emma' (the gunner's name for the 30.5cm) as it was for 'Dicke Bertha'. A shallow pit about twelve feet square was dug and a hoist erected over it. The platform wagon was dragged over the pit, the platform hoisted clear and the wagon removed, and the platform lowered into the pit and levelled. The carriage wagon was then brought up and the weight of the carriage taken by the hoist while the wheels were removed. The carriage was then lowered on to its pivot on the platform and the hoist dismantled. Finally, the howitzer barrel wagon was brought up and the barrel winched from its guides on the wagon into the carriage cradle and connected to the recoil gear. Given a good piece of ground, a well-trained battery could have both guns in action in twenty-four minutes from arriving on the site, and could pack and be ready to move off in forty minutes after firing the last shot.

Offered by the Austro-Hungarian staff, and eagerly accepted by the Germans, a battery of the 30.5 'Emmas' was entrained to Liège and then directed by road to the scene of their first engagement. In conjunction with the Berthas, the 'Emmas' were to attack the fortress of Namur.

Namur was another Liège. The meeting point of six railway lines, it was the pivot of manoeuvre for the French army's plan to retake

Belgium. A ring of nine Brialmont forts, mounting 350 guns between them, encircled the town and lay across the German axis of advance. On 19th August the German thrust arrived, but on this occasion there was no time wasted in trying to 'bounce' a way past; after taking up besieging positions, the troops were put to work levelling sites for the howitzers. By the 21st, both batteries were installed and they immediately opened a bombardment on the three eastern forts – Andoy, Maizeret and Marchovelette.

The following day, the Belgian army mounted a sudden counterattack,

One of the Austrian 30.5cm howitzers takes the road to Namur and Maubeuge

895-847

intent on destroying the four howitzers, but the encircling German line held fast and the attack was thrown back, with heavy casualties to the Belgians. By the 23rd only three forts of the nine were still held, the Belgian army was in retreat, and the Germans entered Namur. The remaining three forts were battered into submission on the 25th, and the howitzers looked round for fresh targets.

They found one at Maubeuge, in north-east France. This important rail junction had been selected as the advanced base of the British Expeditionary Force when plans were drawn up before the war, but before the British could begin to organise there, the German advance was at the gates. Fifteen detached forts with 435 guns surrounded the town, but the reconstruction of these forts on modern lines, though frequently promised, had never been completed, and the heaviest weapons they had were forty-eight 15cm guns.

On 2nd September, the howitzers from Namur, now augmented by another battery of 30.5cm Skodas, were emplaced and began their familiar task. The sites had been carefully selected to the north-east of the fortress, so as to be out of range of the 15cm guns of the defence, and the monotonous success of Liège and Namur was soon repeated. In five days the forts were reduced to ruins or had surrendered, and Maubeuge was in German hands, to remain thus for the rest of the war.

All this furious activity on the part of the German army precipitated the famous 'Retreat from Mons' in which the British regular army held off the weight of the German advance in order to buy yet more time for the French to reorganise and prepare a counterstroke. During the retreat, the disciplined rapid rifle fire of the British infantry tore holes in each German attack, convincing many

The remains of a two-gun turret in one of the Maubeuge forts

Germans that the BEF were more numerous and better armed than they in fact were. This belief was due primarily to the British Lee-Enfield rifle, and its unique bolt-action which could be manipulated faster than any other bolt ever devised and which led the British to perfect a rapid-fire technique which paid off handsomely at Mons.

But these affairs, valiant as they were, have tended to overshadow the action of the artillery during the retreat. From contemplating howitzers firing shells of a ton or so, we now turn to contemplate a gun which weighed rather less than one of Bertha's shells; the British Horse Artillery 13-pounder, 1,184lbs complete, firing a 12½lb shell.

On 1st September, near Compiègne the 1st Cavalry Brigade of the British Expeditionary Force were covering the retreat of III Corps. 'L' Battery of the Royal Horse Artillery and its six horse-drawn 13-pounders had pulled into the village of Néry on the previous night, the last of the brigade units to arrive, and had bivouacked in a field to the south of the village. They were given orders to block two roads running east and south from the village, get what sleep they could, and be ready to move off at 0430 next morning. But 1st September broke with a mist which limited visibility to no more than 200 yards, and although at the appointed time 'L' battery was limbered up and ready to go, orders came to wait until 0500 to see if the weather cleared. The gunners took advantage of the half-hour respite to unhitch their horses and water them nearby, and to try and organise themselves some breakfast.

At 0500, just as the gunners had finished hitching up and were awaiting the order to move, a German shell burst over the village, and a furious gun and rifle fire opened up from some high ground to the east. The pursuing German army had caught up with the retreating brigade, and, being above the mist, had been able to take up good firing positions and totally

'J' Battery, Royal Horse Artillery in position in late 1914

surprise the British troops.

The first result of the uproar was a stampede of cavalry horses down the main street of the village, and as this raging throng galloped madly between the houses a high explosive shell burst among them, effectively blocking the road with dead and dying horses. On the battery bivouac area the gunners, standing around in groups talking and smoking, were rudely disturbed when the shrapnel balls began to whistle past them. A Captain Bradbury gave the immortal cry 'Who's for the guns?' and led a rush to the parked weapons. While horse-holders struggled with the teams, three guns were unhooked and dropped into action facing the direction of the attack; the ammunition was on battery wagons across the other side of the field, and men began to run across the bullet-swept ground with rounds of ammunition tucked under

their arms, sprinting for their lives to give the guns their rations.

Almost as soon as the uneven fight began, one of the three guns took a direct hit from a high explosive shell and was smashed beyond repair. The other two carried on the duel. Two German batteries were opposing them – eight guns – one battery firing on the village, and one devoting all its energy to finishing off 'L' Battery. In a few more minutes a second direct hit ended the career of the second 13-pounder, and Captain Bradbury, assisted by Sergeant Nelson, were left as ˙ gunlayers on the third gun. Survivors of the other gun joined them, and a supply of ammunition was kept up by other members of the battery running between the gun and the wagons; as a runner went down, another took his place.

It was said afterwards that the gun seemed to bear a charmed life; shells burst all around it but it sustained only minor damage. The fire now became even more intense, since the

German battery which had originally been dealing with the village had turned and joined in to try and crush this persistent gadfly of a 13-pounder.

But gradually the fire of the lone British gun began to take effect, and the German gunners began to suffer: the odds were in their favour though, and even if the gun bore a charmed life, the men who served it were only mortal. Lieutenant Mundy, who had been directing fire, was seriously wounded, as was Sergeant Nelson. The ammunition runners had been decimated, for it was now after 0700 hours, and the battle had raged for over two hours. Now Battery-Sergeant-Major Dorrell ran up to assist on the gun, and, as he arrived, Captain Bradbury put him into the layer's post and ran off to fetch ammunition. Within yards he was struck and mortally wounded.

The Sergeant-Major and the wounded Sergeant used up what ammunition was lying around the gun, and that was that; no ammunition, nobody to go for more, nothing left. And then, at the proverbial eleventh hour, as the last shot was fired and the last empty case flung aside, a cavalry charge swooped past them: relief had at last arrived, and the valiant stand of 'L' at Néry had staved off the German advance.

The casualty list was a sorry sight. Forty-five men had been killed or wounded out of a strength of 170. Captain Bradbury, Sergeant-Major Dorrell and Sergeant Nelson were each awarded the Victoria Cross, Bradbury's being posthumous, and rarely were VCs so hardly earned; for this was no momentary flash of bravery, but sustained cold courage against impossible odds for over two hours.

'L' Battery today bear the official Honour Title of 'L' (Néry) Battery, RHA; the gun that served so valiantly on that day was brought back to England and placed in the Imperial War Museum where it remained on show for many years. Recently it has been loaned back to its original owners, so that 'L' proudly exhibits its Néry Gun, and every year celebrates the day when it 'stood alone' against the German army.

By the end of 1914 the skirmishing and open warfare were over. In constant attempts to outflank each other the German and Allied forces had now reached the North Sea on one flank and the Swiss border on the other, and the trenches began to proliferate. The war began to take on the shape it was to retain for almost another four years. It seemed likely that, provided the defences did not get too thick, it might yet be possible to get through them, and for this it appeared most profitable to try and amass whatever artillery was available and concentrate it on the attack front, which, after all, was not a very novel idea. But the concept was now taken a stage further, and it was decided that instead of just putting the guns there and letting them play by ear, a score would be written and the whole ensemble would perform in concert.

The Battle of Neuve Chapelle broke new ground in many ways. It was the first major attack against a trench position, the first of innumerable assaults against earthwork and barbed wire. It was the biggest battle in terms of troops and formations employed which had yet been fought, and, because of this, the British had their hands full trying to control and administer the complete army corps plus a variety of attached troops. But most of all it was the first time such a vast amount of artillery had been collected together and pointed under rigid control at one target. An artillery timetable was conceived in which every gun and howitzer was given a specific task to perform and a time to perform it. 340 guns were assembled for this attack, from 13-pounder field guns to the four 9.2-inch howitzers and solitary 15-inch howitzer that the British army then owned, the latter having been 'donated' by its manufacturer along with its commander and thirty-five shells.

A British 18-pounder gun in action

It is worth pausing to contemplate the 15-inch howitzer; this had been made by the Coventry Ordnance Works more or less as a speculative venture, as a straight scale-up of their 9.2-inch model. For reasons which are not very clear, even today, the Admiralty took the weapon up and it went to France under their auspices, commanded by Admiral Bacon, a naval eminence who had retired and was now a director of the Ordnance Works. But for the sake of convention Admiral Bacon became Colonel Bacon while he commanded the gun. Having performed useful work with it, and made his point about his fitness to return to harness, he later resumed his blue uniform and became Admiral once more, commanding the famous Dover Patrol until the end of 1917.

The remaining guns of the Neuve Chapelle line-up were largely elderly 4.7-inch guns, some 6-inch 30cwt howitzers, 4.5-inch howitzers and 5-inch guns. The 4.7-inch guns were Boer War veterans, though mounted on the improved carriages. The whole assembly of ordnance worked out at one gun for every four yards of attacking front, a concentration which was far beyond anything which had been attempted before.

It was intended that the guns should move into position well ahead of the attack, and range at odd times over a period of days in order to calculate their firing data, so as not to reveal their concentration or targets by doing all their ranging at once. The plan worked well, except that two batteries of 6-inch howitzers which were being sent from England were delayed on their journey and arrived only on the day before the attack was due to begin. Denied the chance to fire ranging shots, they were forced to fire their part of the plan 'off the

'Mother', the original 9.2-inch howitzer, being emplaced before the Battle of Neuve Chapelle

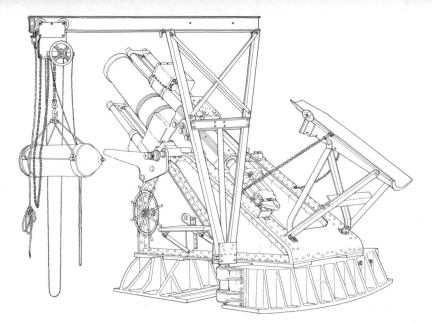

British 15-inch howitzer. 'Granny', the 15-inch howitzer produced by the Coventry ordnance works for the Admiralty on Churchill's order. Eight of these were made and sent to France, but ten thousand yards range was a poor reward for the efforts needed to emplace them

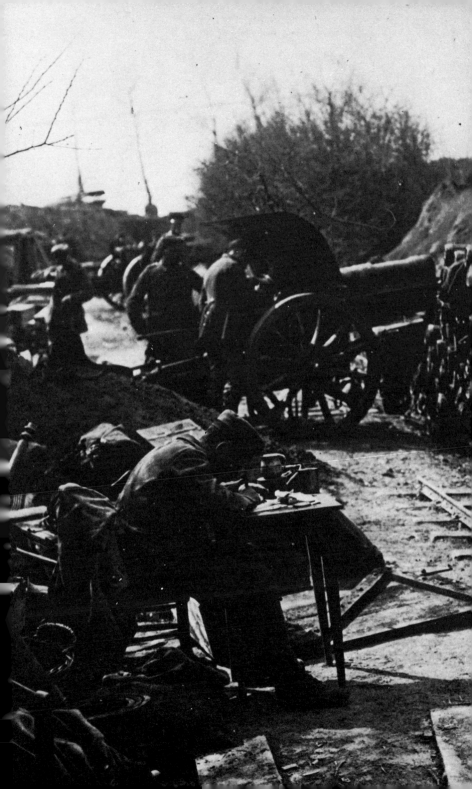

map', that is by plotting their own position on the map, plotting the target, and then measuring the range and bearing between the two. While theoretically sound enough, in 1915 this system was full of hazards. In the first place the maps were not perfectly accurate; in the second place locating a point on the map when that point is in enemy territory is a difficult task. Furthermore, not enough was known or understood at that time about the vagaries of a shell's flight when exposed to wind, temperature changes, barometric pressure and other variables. Today, worked out with computers, this problem still has its drawbacks; in 1915, calculated by a tired soldier with a blunt pencil and a wet finger, it was dangerous.

The artillery timetable finally issued to the guns showed three specific phases of attack. Firstly, the preliminary bombardment of the German trench system, intended to kill the defenders and break down the wire entanglements. Secondly, the bombardment of the rear trench lines, in which the fall of shot would be moved back progressively to land on the rear trenches while the British assault overran the first line. Lastly, a covering bombardment of Neuve Chapelle village, intended to prevent reinforcements upsetting the consolidation by a counterattack.

At 0700 hours on 10th March, the guns fired a few ranging shots to check the effect of weather conditions on the data they had previously deduced from their ranging. If a bearing of 185 degrees and a range of 5,500 yards was required to hit a certain tree-stump in the distance, and if that morning shot showed a need to set $184\frac{1}{2}$ degrees and 5,575 yards on the sights to hit it, then all the data deduced for the attack supporting fire would be corrected by half a degree and seventy-five yards, and would thus fall in the

A German 15cm howitzer battery comfortably settled in position in a sunken road

right places. This need to check was unfortunate, because it awoke the German defenders. They were pretty sure that an attack was forthcoming, and wanted to turn their own artillery loose, a proceeding which would have had fatal results on the occupants of the British front-line trenches, where infantrymen were now packed shoulder to shoulder awaiting the order to go over the top. But it seems that it needed the corps commander's order to permit the guns to fire, and nobody wanted to be the one who had to wake him up and ask him.

Having made the necessary corrections, the bombardment began with a crash at 0730 hours, and the massed guns rained shells on the surprised defenders – surprised not at being attacked, but by the intensity of the fire they were receiving, for this was the heaviest artillery bombardment ever fired in warfare up to that date. The dirt and smoke flung up from the target area mixed with the early morning mist, and soon the visibility was so bad that artillery observation was impossible.

For thirty-five minutes the ground heaved and quaked under an explosive deluge, and then at 0805 the bombardment stopped, lifted, and began to hammer the rear German trench lines as the infantry leaped from their long wait and dashed for the German front line. The wire had been ripped and blasted aside, the trenches battered out of shape, and those defenders who remained alive were so dazed from the bombardment that the first objectives were taken with little or no opposition. Except for one area, the northern sector, where the two 6-inch howitzer batteries were firing. Their map-shooting had been imperfect and the trenches were relatively undamaged so that the attackers there had to fight a determined and well-entrenched enemy.

Once the first trenches were secured, the bombardment entered its third phase of lifting once more to descend on Neuve Chapelle. The assaulting

troops now moved forward to deal with the remaining trench lines, but the bombardment here had been of shorter duration and lesser intensity. The defenders were less shaken, the protecting wire less cut and damaged, and the fight became more difficult.

Eventually, the attack reached its objectives and now the artillery changed once more and brought in a new innovation – a barrage. This was the first time the word had been used, and here it meant exactly what it said, since the fire was a three-sided box of shrapnel which walled off Neuve Chapelle and prevented the entry of German reinforcements while the British infantry dug in.

As far as the artillery was con-

cerned, Neuve Chapelle ended there. But for the infantry the trouble was only just beginning: reinforcements which should now have appeared and driven through them into the German rear area, had failed to materialise. The principal reason was the difficulty of communication in those pre-radio days; to send a message back several miles by runner to tell the reinforcements to move, to get them moving, and then to march them from their location across the shell-torn landscape, took so long that the German defenders rallied, counterattacked, and generally undid most of the work of the morning attack.

But the artillery preparation had been thorough and efficient, and it

German retaliatory fires bursting behind the British trenches at Neuve Chapelle

was unfortunate that the wrong lessons were read from it. Because the outward and visible sign of the artillery's work was torn wire and damaged trenches, it became a solemn belief that to defeat an entrenched position it was necessary to pour on shells until nothing remained standing. The vital point – the intensity of fire which demoralised the men themselves – was overlooked, and it took a long time for the wrong lesson to be unlearned and the right one deduced.

They don't grow on trees

In the present-day climate of management consultancy, cost-effectiveness, work study and other fashionable tribal cries, one subject which exercises the minds of military planners is the provision of a suitable stock-pile of weapons with which to face the prospect of war. No one in his right mind would set forth to wage war without an assured supply of armaments behind him, you might think, but in fact there was a time when several people did just that, and the time in question was August 1914. It is the memory of those early days of war which, even now, arise to haunt procurement officers in the quiet hours of the night.

It must be remembered that previous wars had, by modern standards, been leisurely affairs. Even the Franco-Prussian War, which was by way of being a *blitzkrieg* of its day, moved so slowly between actions that the manufacture of munitions to resupply the armies was relatively simple (al-

though the lessons were discernable in the latter part of the 1870 affair for anyone who took the trouble to find them). One built up one's stock of weapons in peacetime – and these had a long life since design was relatively simple and robust – and the pace of warfare was such that the initial stockpile would take a long time to be devoured, and the all-government manufacturing resources could keep up a steady supply without even demanding much overtime from the workers. So in 1914 the stocks held by the combatants were considered adequate for what promised to be a short war, and everyone was quite convinced that the system would suffice. There was to be a rude awakening.

In the first place, design was beginning to move faster; guns which were in the forefront of technology in 1900 were almost obsolete by 1914, and the new weapons which the European nations had developed in the early years of the century were not available in large enough numbers to withstand the attrition which the war produced. Moreover, new designs proved to be less robust than the old; little can go wrong with a bronze muzzle-loader on a wooden carriage, but in a wire-wound breech-loader with a modern recoil system and complex sighting arrangements there is much that can go wrong, and, of course, replacements take longer to manufacture. The figures for the French artillery are illuminating in this respect; they are no better and no worse than any other combatant, but the detail in which they were published in later years makes them particularly appropriate for pointing the lesson.

At the outbreak of war the French field artillery were furnished with 1,011 batteries of four 75mm guns each, and a reserve of 756 guns. This was considered to be more than ample as a reserve, and, on the assumption that a modern war would be over before

production could be put into effect, the French mobilisation plans did not even consider the manufacture of guns during the course of a war. But the hectic actions of the first few months soon saw the reserve depleted, and by the end of September 1914 it was obvious that some more guns would have to be built. The arsenals at St Chamond and Creusot were thereupon called on to make a further eighty guns. In addition to guns, of course, ammunition is needed, and the stock at the outbreak of war was 1,700 rounds per gun, of which 400 were in reserve – indeed, so much were they in reserve that those 400 consisted of empty components held at the arsenals for completion, and were not actually in a condition to be used without considerable work being done on them. That was the plan; the unpleasant fact was that the stock of ammunition per gun was only 1,400 rounds, of which 200 were in the uncompleted state.

During mobilisation plans the government arsenals were called upon to complete the reserve stock at once and then go into production of shells at a rate of 3,600 per day – which means three rounds per gun per day. To make confusion worse confounded, some of the initial gains by the German army put some of the manufacturing sub-contractors out of business, and the production rate was only 700 shells per day. The first flush of action had led to the use of extravagant quantities of ammunition, some batteries firing off as much as 1,000 rounds in a minor engagement, so that by 10th September the total remaining stock in France was down to 500 rounds per gun, including all the reserves. GQG forthwith demanded a production rate of 40,000 shells per day, then increased this figure to 80,000 per day, and before the manufacturers had time to think, finally upped it to 100,000 per day.

Considering that St Chamond and Creusot were the only manufacturing facilities left, and considering that they were already having difficulty in reaching the original planned figure of

French 27cm howitzer on its transport carriages

39 Siege Battery firing its 8-inch howitzers during the Battle of the Somme, August 1916

3,600 per day, it was obvious that something drastic had to be done to even approach the GQG figures. It was clear that the manufacture of munitions would have to be farmed out to people who had never made anything more warlike than stoves or locomotives. Millerand, the War Minister, held a conference in Bordeaux in September, to which he summoned the principal engineering manufacturers and told them that whether they liked it or not, they were going into the ammunition business. But to make what was wanted in the time available and on the machines available meant that the designs had to be modified to suit the manufacturing capabilities and processes. Thus, instead of explosive shell being forged and machined from steel with a tensile strength capable of standing a pressure of 1,400 kilogrammes to the

square centimetre, it was agreed t press shells from bar, cast them from scrap, and adopt other methods whic resulted in a shell which could onl withstand 400 kilogrammes to th square centimetre.

Under such dispensations product ion got under way with remarkabl rapidity, but the price had to be paid and the bill was called due when th ammunition got to the guns. Th reduced specification meant that th shells could barely withstand th firing pressure; with the added hazar of fast filling of low-grade explosive poor inspection and hasty productio more of the shells burst inside th guns than burst on the targets, or s is seemed to the unfortunate gunner The shortage of guns was now mad more acute by the bursting or bulgin of barrels caused by the faulty am munition, and things became ver hazardous for the French artillery.

In order to paper over the gaps an find something to shoot until th replacement guns could be made, i became necessary to scour every corner to find weapons. The French colonies were raided for every field gun they possessed, 65mm mountain guns being sent out to them in their place; antiquated models such as the non-recoil 90mm, the 95mm M1873, and stocks of naval weapons were pulled from store and sent to the front together with their elderly ammunition. Every fort which appeared to be remote from the possibility of action was stripped of what guns could be taken without actually having to dismantle the building to get at them. Although there was a dire shortage of heavy guns as well as field guns, GQG refused to make any remark on the supply of heavier weapons until the field gun supply was assured, which had the benefit of leaving the manufacturers in peace to get on with providing 75mm guns as fast as they could; but for all their endeavours, it was the latter half of 1915 before the flow from the factories assumed satisfactory proportions.

A return of gun losses dated 1st January 1916 gives some revealing figures: up to that date 1,000 guns had been blown up due to faulty ammunition, 600 sufficiently damaged from the same cause to be made unserviceable until rebuilt, 750 had been discarded after they had been worn out from firing, and 400 had been either captured or destroyed by the enemy. In sixteen months, the French had lost over twice as many 75s as they had started out with. The same return rendered on 1st January 1917 was even more sombre: 1,100 blown up, 2,700 damaged, 2,250 worn out and 1,200 ineffective due to enemy action. How could supplies stand up to this fearful rate of attrition?

By the middle of 1915 only sixty new guns, of any calibre, had been made; the soldiers were hanging on by the skin of their teeth, using museum pieces turned out of dark corners and redundant forts. But that was the turning-point. By the end of the year 2,010 were supplied; then 4,550 in 1916,

5,400 in 1917 and 6,350 in 1918. So that by the latter days of 1915 the supply problem for 75mm guns had been solved, and from then on supply could always beat demand. But as the Duke of Wellington once remarked 'It was a damned close-run thing'. By the end of 1915 all antedeluvian artillery had been withdrawn, and only the modern designs were in use at the front.

Ammunition too, after its shaky start, was soon coming forth in volume, but the quality was not all that it might have been until well into 1917, as the figures quoted above for gun accidents show. One of the factors which made this worse was that the changing character of the war caused a greater demand for high explosive shell than for shrapnel, and HE shell is the more touchy proposition. More or less any competent company can make shrapnel shells and if they do turn out a faulty one, a burst in the gun barrel will do no harm. But a high explosive shell is a more difficult manufacturing task in some respects, and faults manifest themselves in an unmistakeable fashion, destroying the guns and probably half the detachment too.

The mobilisation plan called for production of 409,000 shells a month; in fact, October 1914 saw the actual output figure down to 250,000 shells and 140,000 shrapnel, a total of 390,000, and November's production figures were even lower. But from this low water mark the figures began to take an upswing until in May 1917 over 7,000,000 shells were supplied – seventeen times the mobilisation plan figure. And for the record, a grand total of 208,265,000 75mm shells were turned out between 1st August 1914 and 1st November 1918 – 126,500 shells per day, about thirty-five times the planned figure.

In the heavy artillery class, as has been noted, GQG had the good sense to hold off the demands until the field gun programme was settled and producing results. It then sat down to see what was wanted and find out what

could be done about it. The stock held by the army at the outbreak of war was some 300 weapons, and due to the mobile nature of the early battles, few of them were deployed in positions of danger and fewer still lost to the enemy. Orders had been placed at the outbreak of war for 220 105mm guns to be delivered forthwith, 120 155mm guns to be delivered during 1917 and eighteen 28cm howitzers to be delivered some time in 1916. This order took a back seat when the rush to provide 75s was under way, and replacements were supplied by the same system as had helped out the field gunners – raiding forts, naval stocks, and siege train stocks, producing railway and other improvised mountings to get them to where the action was. There were also a number of weapons held by makers which had been produced for foreign orders, and these peacetime contracts were now sequestered and taken into French service, as well as a number of weapons which the manufacturers had

made speculatively and which the were now delighted to sell to th army. This all meant a proliferatio of odd calibres and miscellaneou equipment, but it was tolerated unde the circumstances, and at least ther were enough guns to be going on with

By the middle of 1915, with the fiel gun programme running smoothly GQG reorganised the heavy artiller by standardising on five weapons an discarding the odd assortment c guns scraped together in 1914. The had begun to realise that the way th war was going, more and more heav artillery would be needed, so th opportunity was taken to get it righ from the start. Even so, a good dea of argument raged back and fort and several commissions sat ar deliberated before, in August 1916, th rationalised programme was declare This demanded the production c 4,800 weapons of 105mm, 155mn 220mm and 280mm calibres. Not wai ing for the official announcemen GQG had already ordered some

Above left : One of the elderly 155mm guns with which the French fought tenaciously while awaiting the production of new designs. Note the wheel ramps to return the carriage to place after each shot. *Above :* The 155mm Schneider gun being brought into action ; the barrel is being winched into place. *Below :* German troops examine a captured French 28cm howitzer. This is a fortress weapon pressed into field service, as can be seen by the heavy ground mounting

Above : French 22cm howitzer ; another piece of position pressed into more mobile duties. *Below :* Another view of the 155mm Schneider gun being prepared for firing. The barrel is about to be assembled to the carriage

them, so that the 105mm M1913, 155mm M1915 and 280mm howitzers were already in production, and plans were well advanced for the production of the other two, the 155mm gun and the 220mm gun. By the latter half of 1917, all these weapons were more or less in volume production, and by April 1918 a return to GQG on the programme showed that of the 4,800 demanded, 3,070 had been supplied, the balance being made up from obsolescent models which were gradually being replaced; by the end of 1918, in fact, all the old models had gone and the heavy gun strength was 5,970, all in the recommended models.

The heavy ammunition supply problem was much the same story as that for the field guns, but with less urgency about it; mobilisation plans called for no more than 465 rounds per day for the 155mm gun to be produced, and nothing for any other weapon, since peacetime stocks were expected to cover any eventuality. In fact, stocks of heavy ammunition were quite respectable, some 5,000,000 rounds being held. So there was not so much desperation as there had been in the case of the 75mm supply, and the lessons learned in that programme were studied before work began on augmenting the heavy supply. The long run of premature explosions with hastily manufactured 75mm shells was sufficient warning; a 75mm premature is bad enough, but a 28cm premature could be catastrophic; and moreover there were not so many heavy guns that they could afford to blow them up at the rate suffered by the 75s. Thus, the shell designs were carefully modified; there was to be no concession to allow makers to adopt doubtful manufacturing methods, no boring from bar or cold pressing. As a minor concession, they were allowed to make them from cast iron instead of steel, but only when the design had been altered to provide an acceptable safety factor. This meant that the shell wall was thicker and thus there was less room

for high explosive inside the shell, and so the effect on the enemy was diminished. This in turn led to firing more ammunition in order to get the necessary effect, so the whole thing became a vicious circle. It was decided to break it by using cast steel, an improvement over cast iron but not so good as wrought steel, and production of shells of this material began in early 1915, and by mid-1916 cast iron shells were abandoned.

The engineering problem of producing vast numbers of shells – for by August 1918 the monthly production was running at 881,000 high explosive, 210,000 shrapnel and 60,000 gas-filled shells – were formidable enough, but an even bigger problem was the provision of the explosives to put inside them. Like most countries at that time, France was dependent upon the German chemical industry for the bulk of the raw materials used in explosive manufacture, and because of this very large stocks were held for war emergency use. It was assumed that these stocks would be sufficient to last through a war, and mobilisation plans did not envisage any increase in production; the three government factories were simply to use up their stocks of materials on hand, and when this ran out it was hoped that the war would end the same day. In the event, one factory at Esquerdez in northern France was abandoned at the outbreak of war and, together with its stock of both finished explosives and raw materials, it fell into German hands. By this time the consumption of shells had been revealed, and GQG were demanding forty tons of high explosive per day for shell filling alone. In order to meet this demand it became necessary to build factories, also to pass some of the burden over to the civil chemical industry and to import material from abroad, both raw chemicals and finished explosives.

At this juncture a few well-meaning inventors and a few out-and-out swindlers got into the act. The latter years of the 19th Century and the opening years of the 20th had seen a vast interest in armaments and explosives and the patent lists were thick with weapons and explosive inventions. One of the very early French adoptions was a substance called 'Turpenite' – from the inventor's name – which was a liquid explosive of doubtful efficiency. What it lacked in chemical power it made up in skilful advertisement, and before long it was being noised about in the newspapers as the final answer to all problems. It was alleged that this liquid was so potent that what it failed to demolish by its detonating force it finished off with its fumes, and thereby it started the poison-gas alarm of 1914 among the Germans. But Turpenite was merely a stop-gap which had been accepted for use when the safer and more conventional explosives were in short supply, and by the spring of 1915 the Turpenite shell was a thing of the past. It would be interesting to know just how many of the 75s which blew up due to faulty ammunition were victims of Turpenite, even without the added complication of poor manufacture and poor shell body material.

In 1917 a combine calling itself the 'White Power Syndicate' was busily engaged in trying to promote a new and powerful explosive (all new explosives are powerful) called 'Halakite' to the War Departments of the British and French governments. They also made approaches to the Russian government, in which they went so far as to state that this explosive was being used as a shell filling by the British. The British Ministry of Munitions had examined a sample of Halakite but, not being very impressed, and not getting any very forthright answers about its composition or manufacture from the

German 10cm gun M 1914, a weapon which could out-perform most of its competitors

promoters, it had, very properly, refused them the necessary facilities to open a factory for its manufacture. Unfortunately the Syndicate, like many before it, had taken the trouble to interest one or two honest men – who were virtually acting as a front – and one of these, convinced that the stuff was of value and that the government was missing out on the deal, took the step of voicing his complaints in a newspaper. This brought him afoul of the Official Secrets Act, but it also afforded the authorities a chance to promote a public enquiry into the activities of the Syndicate and the virtues or otherwise of Hala-

French 24cm howitzer of an early type in action in December 1916. An attempt to improve on this led to massive technical problems

Breech mechanism and sights of the German 10cm M 1914

kite. The reports of the Commission, were it not for the sombre background of the war, would make amusing reading. 'The explosive in question was consistent only in name, since the various samples of it which have been submitted differed materially in composition, and in one case at least contained nitro-glycerine, the one substance which the Syndicate had affirmed NOT to be present . . . The French and Russian governments were told . . . that a fully equipped works was engaged in its manufacture, whereas, outside samples, a sardine-tin would hold the entire output.' A Professor of Chemistry attending as an expert witness declared 'The compounding together of the ingredients named cannot yield an explosive material of any value . . . and the specification is the production of charlatans who seek to conceal the worthless nature of their invention by the use of scientific terminology.' The samples submitted were then assessed: 'It has now been shown that all the samples of Halakite presented to the Court contained manufactured cordite as the common ingredient. It is in fact a standard military propellant powder contaminated by the addition of undesirable impurities. A fraud was perpetrated by the proprietors of Halakite, and the clumsy nature of the fraud was obvious to the British and French authorities concerned in the negotiations.'

The well-meaning figureheads were gently rebuked for their enthusiasm for such a cause, and Halakite was heard of no more; strangely, I can find no record of criminal proceedings being taken against the instigators of the fraud.

But in spite of such sidelines, by early 1917 the French government had twelve factories producing explosives and another dozen private firms had gone into the business, to such an extent that although the maximum capacity of the industry was now 985 tons per day, that figure was never reached, the highest output coming in the latter days of 1917 with an output of 870 tons a day including blasting explosives.

A more difficult problem was the supply of the propellant to send the shell on its way, and here the French were in a peculiar position. For many years the production of smokeless powder in France had been a government monopoly – this covered every application, not just artillery ammunition; even the farmer with his shotgun was dependent upon government powder. This caused a good deal of bitterness among French sportsmen who were quite convinced that the stuff was inferior to powders enjoyed by foreigners – for the monopoly went so far as to prohibit the importation of smokeless powder into France. This was no doubt most remunerative during peacetime, but they were in a dangerous position when the demands of war were voiced.

In 1914 there were six factories producing artillery powder, with a grand total output between them of fifteen tons a day. The mobilisation plans called for a speeding up to a rate of forty tons a day in two months. This of course, like every other figure, was soon upset. Although they did the impossible and were producing fifty tons a day by the end of the year, this was inadequate, and new factories were needed. Four were to be built, with a target output which would give an overall production of 500 tons a day. But, of course, these factories could not spring into being overnight, and the production of smokeless powder was a long and tedious process; it would be mid-1916 before any of these four factories produced a single grain, so it became necessary to repeal the ban on importation and import in bulk. In October 1914 an order went to the USA for 3,000 tons of powder to be delivered in 1915, but this was unrealistic, for no factory in the United States was prepared for production

at such a rate. Once deliveries did start, the U-boats took their toll of the traffic, and it was 1916 before the imports began to build up into the bulk demanded. Eventually about a quarter of all the French smokeless powder was being provided from the USA; the new factories never achieved their target figures, the maximum deliveries being in the order of 400 tons a day in late 1917.

As already stated, similar tales can be gleaned from British or German gun and ammunition figures. Indeed, the British experience was a good deal more traumatic; the politicians made meat of the shortages and the affair known as the 'Shells Scandal' was blazoned in the press.

The root of the 'Shells Scandal' lay in the British Equipment Tables which laid down the proportion of shrapnel shell and high explosive shell allotted to the various natures of artillery. The British artillery was thoroughly shrapnel-oriented in prewar days, the use of high explosive shell being confined to coast artillery and field howitzers of the heavier nature. Even so, every gun or howitzer was provided with shrapnel, even the 12-inch and 13.5-inch coast guns (against the chance of an enemy attempting a landing from boats within their range). But once the war settled down in France it was found that the high explosive shell was more valuable than the shrapnel when attacking an entrenched enemy, and consequently more and more battery commanders began demanding increased supplies of high explosive shell. The laid-down proportion of HE shells for the field artillery was a smaller percentage than shrapnel, and this had been the guiding figure in allotting production, so the lack of shells was beginning to be felt by early 1915, indeed it was beginning to put a damper on action. The supply situation was geared to turn out eight HE shells per 18-pounder gun per day, but the demand at the front was now reaching 100 a

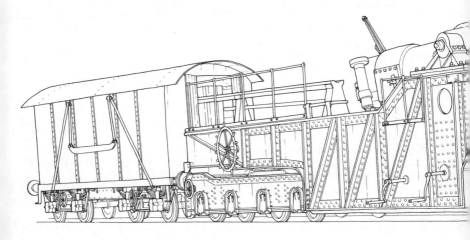

British 12-inch railway gun mark 9. Only two of these weapons were made. The first, made in 1915 by Vickers, had a different wheel arrangement to that shown here which is the second gun, made in 1916 by the Elswick ordnance company

The first British 12-inch railway gun fires, near Maricourt in late 1916. The gun detachment seem unconcerned, in contrast with the spectators

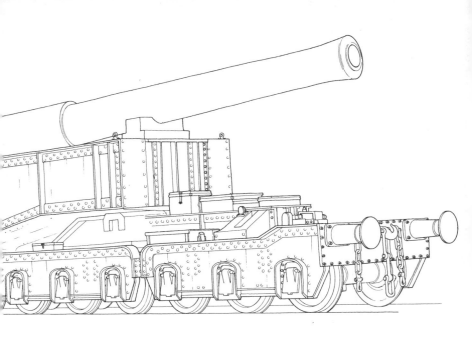

day, even when no major action was going on. By 1st July 1915 the 18-pounders had only slightly over fifty per cent of their allocation, while other guns had even less.

Even the most way-out 'quick-firing' maniacs had never suspected that ammunition would be devoured in quantities like this, but as soon as the tendency had revealed itself, the army had taken steps to do something about it. Major-General von Donop, Master-General of the Ordnance, vastly increased the ammunition contracts and brought many civilian firms into the munitions field, but all this took time to develop. Moreover, peacetime habits died hard; workers were disinclined to work night shifts, so for half the time the factories stood idle. Trade Unions bitterly resented what they termed 'dilution of labour' and clung to every restrictive practice hallowed by time so as to safeguard their position. Either a massive change of heart or of legislation would be needed to correct the malaise, and neither appeared likely. The workers were unlikely to change, since the war was a long way off and there was no apparent urgency; and the army had to take what it was offered, since it had no powers to do anything else about it.

This stalemate was rudely blown apart by the Fourth Estate. For some time, returning soldiers had spoken of shortages – not only of ammunition – at the front, and rumour was afoot. In April, Asquith, speaking at Newcastle-on-Tyne – home of the Elswick Ordnance Company, one of the greatest armament concerns – strongly denied any shortages: 'There is not a word of truth in the statement,' he said, and went on to castigate the rumour-mongers.

Nowadays, of course, we are a good deal less trusting of the statements of politicians, and the instant reaction to that sort of remark would be to take it as an affirmative that there was a shortage of monumental proportions. But in 1915 people still believed what they heard, and the panic died down.

Colonel Charles A'Court Repington had entered the Rifle Brigade in 1878 and served with distinction in Afghanistan, Burma and the Sudan. He retired from active service in 1902 and joined *The Times* as Military Critic and Correspondent, and in that capacity went to France as soon as War Correspondents were permitted there. By virtue of his years in the service he had acquaintances all through the army, and was able to get about and talk to people to probably a greater degree than any of his contemporaries. At the time of the Battle of Aubers Ridge in May 1915 he was staying with General Sir John French, Commander of the British Expeditionary Force. French was severely critical of the ammunition shortage which, he contended, had contributed to the failure of the Aubers attack, and he gave Repington facts and figures. Repington duly wrote a report which spoke plainly of the shortage of ammunition, and sent it off to *The Times*.

Lord Northcliffe, proprietor of *The Times*, was involved at the time in an agitation to back Lloyd George, Chancellor of the Exchequer, against Lord Kitchener, Secretary of State for War, and Repington's report was grist to the mill. *The Times* and the *Daily Mail* (another Northcliffe newspaper) immediately headlined the report – 'The Shells Scandal – Lord Kitchener's Tragic Blunder' – but Kitchener was high in the esteem of the man in the street, and the campaign misfired.

However, other currents were at play in the murky waters of politics and the upshot was the formation of a Coalition Government on 26th May from which Lloyd George emerged as Minister of Munitions, with a mandate to produce the goods. Sweeping powers to outlaw strikes, prohibit lockouts, take over premises, control profits, and organise shift work were given to the new Ministry and with

Lloyd George, together with M Thomas, the French minister responsible for artillery and munitions supply, and Lord Reading

a flourish a new era of munitions production began.

It made little difference. Lloyd George discovered the same truth that many others were discovering about the same time. Ammunition and guns cannot be called into being by the stroke of a pen and made available for issue overnight. Although new factories were built, workers organised, raw materials furnished, the greatest requirement was time, and until this had been provided the situation remained the same. The programme initiated by General von

Donop began to show results, and from the fruits of this the army began to claw its way back, first to a sufficiency and then to the surplus needed to be able to plan and execute operations. But it was the middle of 1916 before the stocks of ammunition could be adjudged sufficient for the demands of a major operation.

So far we have been considering the supply of guns and munitions of types which were in service when the war broke out, but before the battles had been going very long, demand arose for new kinds of weapon. For example, in October 1914 the British troops were somewhat put out to discover that one of the irritants pointed in their direction was, to quote a contemporary report, 'a small trench howitzer which throws an explosive shell the size of a tennis ball for a range of about six hundred yards'. Immediately, they demanded something of the sort for their own use. The trench mortar, as it came to be known, had made its appearance.

The original German mortar, or *Minenwerfer*, was a simple but effective device. It was a steel tube of 90mm calibre, two feet long, slung into a light steel frame. It had a limited number of elevation angle options, the greatest being but twenty-five degrees, and the bomb was fitted with an 'All-ways' fuze, so that no matter which way it fell, it would go off on impact. The weapon was a breech-loader, though the breech mechanism was of extreme simplicity. Rough as it was, it did what was needed and gave the infantry a useful accretion of firepower without having to send runners back to the artillery when it was needed.

The quick and easy answer to it was to copy it as it stood, and this was what the British did. By Christmas of 1914 a hundred had been made, copied from a captured German model and shipped to France to keep the soldiers happy until something better could be provided. Indeed, some thought on these lines had been voiced

Above left : The original, simple, German *Minenwerfer*. *Above :* The later, less simple, *Minenwerfer*. A rifled muzzle-loader, the gunners had to be precise in fitting the shell into the bore. *Below :* A *Minenwerfer* troop in action

as early as August, and the BEF's request merely speeded things up; by the end of October, while the German copies were being made, a general specification for a trench howitzer had been drawn up and had been circulated to the principal armament companies, with a request that they turn their immediate attention to producing some sort of an answer.

The Germans, too, had realised that they had a likely winner on their hands, and set to work; firstly to increase the number available – only fifty were on hand – and then to develop better models firing bigger shells to a longer range. In the same spirit as moved the British, the call went out to the arms makers, and many responded, mortars of varying degrees of utility and weirdness being produced by Mauser, Lanz, Heidenheim and Ehrhardt, all of much the same simplicity as the original which had been designed and produced by Rhenische Metalwarenfabrik, to become better known in a later war as Rheinmetall.

By the middle of 1915 the British Ordnance Board was knee deep in potential trench mortars. A 4-inch rifled muzzle-loader had been approved and issued; Vickers proposed converting a 75mm howitzer design but were turned down on the grounds that the breech action did not look like being compatible with trench mud; one contractor, Babcock and Wilson the boiler people, very ingeniously converted a 5-inch shell body into a mortar, giving it a 4.5-inch calibre and mounting it on a small steel-plate frame with elevation controlled by a clamp. The most popular idea was the stick bomb, a system which promised a heavy shell from a light gun. A large spherical bomb was attached to a steel or wooden rod of about 2-inch diameter. This was thrust down a 2-inch barrel and a propelling charge fired beneath it. As the stick and bomb left the mortar, the stick acted to keep the projectile stable and helped accuracy. In some models the stick was thrown off after leaving the barrel, but these were turned down as being too dangerous for the firers. 2-inch and 1.75-inch stick bomb mortars were eventually accepted and produced for services.

A feature which attracted the inevitable lunatic fringe was the admirable idea of a flashless, smokeless and noiseless weapon. They had unfortunately not heeded a remark made some years earlier by a well known explosives engineer named Soddy, who sagely stated that the flashless, smokeless, noiseless explosive was usually powerless as well. A rash of compressed air mortars, acetylene mortars, spring catapults and similar devices appeared. Some worked: Lieutenant West's Spring Gun was adopted and used very successfully for throwing heavy grenades. But many did not work, and among this number were the centrifugal guns.

The idea of using centrifugal force to launch missiles crops up from time to time. The general idea is to rotate a disc at high speed and then drop a missile on to it; this is allowed to run out to the edge, gathering the disc's velocity as it goes, and is then released at the edge to fly through the air. One such device submitted in 1915 could throw a 10-pound bomb 150 yards after ten minutes cranking by two men, but to remain steady while it was being cranked, it had to weigh 250lbs and was scarcely a reasonable proposition in a trench.

One ingenious weapon put forward by a naval officer had a heavy bomb in the form of a wheel with a toothed circumference. This was fitted on a shaft and wound up to a high rate of revolution by the usual soldier on the crank, eventually building up, so the inventor claimed, as much as 6,000 foot-tons of energy. The wheel was then released from the shaft and, the teeth giving it grip, would roll rapidly off into the enemy lines, jumping obstacles as it came to them. By this time the Chief Superintendant of Ordnance Factories, who had to pronounce on each and every one of these inventions, vented his impatience with the latest in the long line of unworkable projects: 'It is estimated that, leaving out all allowance for friction, it would take one man sixty-nine hours on the handle to prepare to fire one round . . .' The Ordnance Board appear to have taken the hint, and hand-cranked machines were discouraged from then on.

But by this time the ultimate trench mortar had arrived – from a completely outside source. A Mr Wilfred Stokes, managing director of Ransomes and Rapier, an engineering firm well known for steam engines and agricultural machines, submitted a design of mortar in March 1915. It was a smooth-bore muzzle loader with a barrel about four feet long, weighed thirty-six pounds, and was of 3-inch calibre. The bottom of the barrel fitted into a bedplate, and a light bipod held the tube at the desired elevation. The bomb was a simple cast-iron cylinder filled with gunpowder. Its first demonstration was a *tour de force*. The mortar was relatively smokeless and it was amazingly accurate. The only drawback was that the shell turned end-over-end in the air, which necessitated a time fuse being fitted. If Mr Stokes could perhaps design a shell which landed on its nose, so that we could put a simpler impact fuze in it? Stokes came back four days later with a bomb which landed on its nose.

At this stage the usual arguments began. This department didn't like it because it seemed that it might be dangerous if a bomb stuck in the barrel when loading. Stokes pointed out that there was a difference in diameter between bomb and barrel of a quarter of an inch, and it seemed to him it would need a hell of a lot of

The Stokes 3-inch mortar was also capable of being used in the anti-aircraft role, when fitted with special sights

dirt to wedge the bomb. He eventually lost that argument and redesigned the breech-plug so that the firing pin could be withdrawn to a safe position while the mortar was upended to tip the bomb out. Another department raised objections, so Stokes designed a safety catch. Now came objections to his shells; he had developed a teardrop shaped bomb with four fins – the great-grandfather of practically every mortar bomb designed since – but it was felt that something simpler would fill the bill and be easier for manufacture by firms unused to manufacturing war materials without interfering with scarce supplies and machine tools needed for artillery shells. So a redesign was submitted.

Eventually, in August, everybody was happy and the 3-inch Stokes Mortar was approved, designs sealed, and production got under way. Mr Stokes then got busy again and within a month had a 4-inch mortar, for firing smoke bombs, ready for test. This went much faster, and by October 1915 was in use at the front. Stokes later became Sir Wilfred Stokes, a well-merited recognition of 'the man who put the mortar on the map'.

The mortar business soon began to escalate. If a 3-inch mortar was good, then a 6-inch would be twice as good. So a 6-inch and later a 9.45-inch were developed, and these weapons became an artillery responsibility. They were, on examination, simple muzzle-loading howitzers; their size and weight removed them from the two-men-and-down-the-trench sphere of warfare: they demanded emplacements, proper ammunition supply, fire control, observation posts and all the paraphinalia of the guns. Their sole virtue lay in their high trajectory and ability to drop their enormous shells straight down into a trench at ranges which the 'real' howitzers found too short.

The German Minenwerfer or 'Minnies' went the same way, abandoning the rustic simplicity of 1914 until it became hard to say whether they were mortars or howitzers. Both had recoil

systems, carriages, spades, wheels; except for size, there seemed little to choose between them. The prime virtue of the mortar is epitomised by Stoke's designs; cheapness, lightness, rapidity in action, and, above all, cheap, effective ammunition. These had become lost in the German designs, and with them went the value of the mortar in mobile warfare. But for static warfare as it was from 1915 to 1918, anything went, and so the complication and expense of the heavy mortars was accepted. When the big displacements of 1918 uprooted everybody, the disadvantages of these howitzers was plain to see, and it was noticeable that by the 1930s all these weapons had been swept away in favour of improved versions of Stokes's original pattern.

Another new weapon introduced in 1914 was the anti-aircraft gun. This was a specialised equipment; the gun was fairly standard, but the mounting had to allow for an elevation to eighty

British 6-inch trench mortar. Typical of the 'trench howitzers' the British 6-inch performed well, remaining in reserve stocks until the Second World War. Elevation and traverse are applied by operating the turnscrews on the barrel supports and the bomb was muzzle loaded

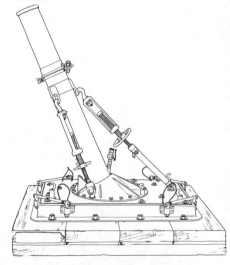

A British 13-pounder 9-cwt
anti-aircraft gun in action,
October 1917

or ninety degrees, it had to have all-round traversing capability, and the sights were a special case. So little was known or surmised about anti-aircraft shooting that anybody who had an idea was welcome. The question of shooting at aircraft had arisen about 1908, when the flying machine began to show military possibilities. In 1909 Krupp and Erhardt both exhibited anti-aircraft guns, the Erhardt being an advanced design mounted on a motor chassis. But no government was ready to plunge into arming the forces with these weapons until some fundamental research had been done, so that when the war began the available anti-aircraft guns were few, ill-adapted to their job, imperfectly understood, and, in general, ineffective. The activities of the early aviators were relatively innocuous, largely confined to reconnaissance, but nevertheless their performance showed that some form of defence against their activities, or at least some method of persuading

them to go away, might be worthwhile after all, and suddenly the anti-aircraft gun was popular.

The British experience might here be taken as fairly representative of all the combatants, beginning with a few purpose-built weapons, expanding into a motley collection of everything which could shoot upwards, then settling eventually into a reasonable armoury of effectives. When the war began, the military had been considering the attack of aircraft for some time, and had performed a good deal of quiet basic research into such questions as to whether HE, Shrapnel or some other type of shell was best; whether percussion fuzes or time fuzes should be used; what type of sight was most effective, and so on. The weapons actually in service were firstly about 50 one-pounder 'pom-pom' guns, belt-fed weapons resembling an over-

77

grown Maxim gun, which had first forced themselves into prominence due to their use by the Boers in South Africa. This experience led to their adoption in the British army on a two-wheeled carriage as a sort of rapid-fire field-piece. In 1909 some of these were taken from this carriage and placed on a static mounting for use in defending ports and dockyards. They were scattered about in existing forts and became a Garrison Artillery responsibility, much as anti-aircraft defence fell to the lot of the Coast Artillery in the United States Army at the same period.

The second weapon available was a heavier gun, designed to deal with the potential threat of the airship – the Zeppelin. This was a 3-inch gun; there were already a number of guns of this calibre in British service, so to avoid confusion, since the gun barrel and breech weighed exactly one ton, it became known as the 3-inch 20cwt. This could also be mounted on a pedestal, for static defences, and could reach up to 19,000 feet with a shrapnel shell. The policy was to sit tight in the static defence and let the airship come to you; the odds were that he would get lost *en route*, or get blown off course, so there was little point in looking for him.

But guns sunk in concrete surrounding Portsmouth Dockyard are small consolation to an Expeditionary Force in France, and by September 1914 the designers were hard at work again, manufacturing some sort of mobile carriage on which the pom-pom and the 3-inch '20' could be slung to take them to France. The pom-pom was a simple proposition. The original two-wheel carriage was modified to allow the gun to reach eighty degrees elevation, and that was that. The 3-inch was a little more difficult, but the designers came up with a simple answer which became the ancestor of practically every anti-aircraft gun which followed it. A plain square steel platform carried four legs, one at each corner. These

The Zeppelin – not such an easy target as was first supposed

could be hinged up, and two wheels hooked on to each end for moving. The 3-inch pedestal mount was unbolted from its concrete and bolted straight on to the platform, and that was that. Towed into place by any available tractor, the wheels were removed, the legs lowered, screwjacks applied to level it, and the gun was in business.

In September 1914, though, and for several months after that, it did not need many fingers to count the number of 3-inch '20s' available, and the search was on for something to fill the gap. The French were using their 75mm field gun, placing it on a high angle mounting on a motor truck. Thus the British 13-pounder field gun suddenly found itself modified into an anti-aircraft gun. The modifications were simple – a spring catch was fitted in the breech so that when loaded at a high angle the cartridge did not fall out before the breech block was closed, and an extra strong return spring was fitted into the recoil system to haul the gun back up the steep angle after recoil. Fitted onto a Packard chassis it became a light and mobile weapon; for the tactic of anti-aircraft gunnery had taken a fresh turn. The policy now was to have groups of the mobile mountings located in barracks at various places – notably around London – ready, like fire engines, to turn out when the alarm was sounded. The civil police acted as a warning system, and a series of telephone calls from village policemen would soon indicate the path of an oncoming raider, so that the nearest mobile battery would turn out and position itself in the predicted path.

While the raider was the ponderous airship, moving at about 60mph, this system was reasonably efficient, but

Part of the London defences; a 75mm M 1897 gun on a pivoting platform

Above: The French auto-cannon, a 75mm anti-aircraft gun on a motor mounting
Below: The Horse Artillery's 13-pounder mounted on a truck to become an anti-aircraft gun

the speed of raiders soon increased, and it became apparent that permanent siting was the only answer. This, of course, demanded more guns, and the lash-up kings had a field-day. The 13-pounder was given a longer barrel so as to produce a higher velocity; the 18-pounder was similarly cannibalised into a high-angle role, but only in small numbers, for this gun was now the backbone of the army in France. Spare naval and coast defence 4-inch and 4.7-inch guns, held in store as replacements for shipboard armament, were withdrawn, modified to elevate to the necessary angles and emplaced. Even such wildly improbable weapons as 6-inch howitzers, 7.5-inch guns, 12-pounders and 6-inch QF guns were all pressed into the defence of London. Armament manufacturers turned out their stores and sent along anything which could be elevated, while stocks of guns intended for foreign buyers were taken over whenever they could be made to shoot upwards. The Elswick Ordnance Company had ten 3-inch 10-pounder

guns it had built for a Russian battleship; the battleship was not ready and was not likely to be for some time, so the guns went off to the Royal Navy. They were not sure about them, and with a burst of goodwill, presented them to the army, who spent six months trying to fit them onto some form of mobile mount, then gave up and handed them back to the navy. Their eventual fate is unrecorded.

Concurrent with the problem of producing guns came the problem of getting the gun to damage the target. The first ideas on this subject envisaged using tracer shells so that the flight could be seen and visually corrected on to the target. The gunlayer would use a simple open sight capable of being offset to 'aim off' to compensate for the movement of the target. Once fire was opened a simple observation of the path of the tracer would allow an observer to make the necessary corrections to bring fire on to the target. This system worked very well on experimental ranges, where highly-skilled observers could

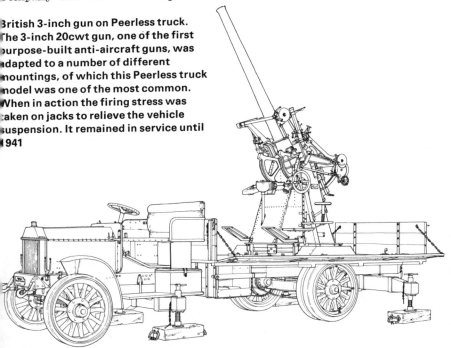

British 3-inch gun on Peerless truck. The 3-inch 20cwt gun, one of the first purpose-built anti-aircraft guns, was adapted to a number of different mountings, of which this Peerless truck model was one of the most common. When in action the firing stress was taken on jacks to relieve the vehicle suspension. It remained in service until 1941

The field artillery's 18-pounder was provided with a special carriage to become an anti-aircraft gun, but this idea was not a success

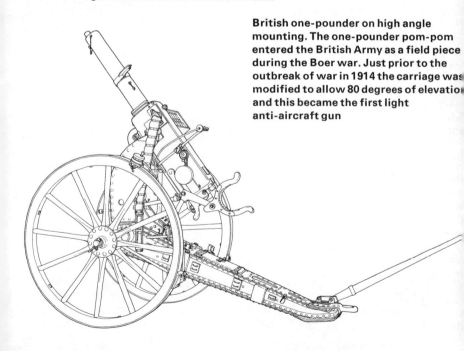

British one-pounder on high angle mounting. The one-pounder pom-pom entered the British Army as a field piece during the Boer war. Just prior to the outbreak of war in 1914 the carriage was modified to allow 80 degrees of elevation and this became the first light anti-aircraft gun

e spread about, but in practice it roved hopeless. The curving path of he trajectory was most deceptive, nd shooting by this system owed nore to luck than to good judgement.

Thus the business of fire control volved into three parts: first, to ositively locate the target in space; econd, to calculate how long the shell vould take to get up there; and third o predict where the target would e by the time the shell arrived. Once these three considerations had een dealt with, it became necessary o juggle with the second and third arts until shell and target appeared o occupy the same place at the same ime, which was the object of the alculation. But this sort of calcula- ion cannot be done on the fingers, nd many and various slide rules, raphs, tables, and patent sights were onstructed to do the task and do it efore the target got tired of waiting nd went home. One drawback was he demand for a squad of mathema- icians around every gun, doing sums, eading graphs, setting sights, calcu- ating fuse lengths and getting in each ther's way. In order to economise in rain-power and let the gunners get n with shooting, the next step was o concentrate the arithmetic in the niddle of a group of guns, and then ass the answer out to all of them. After several devices had been tried, French inventor, Brocq, devised his Central Post Instrument', or 'Tachy- neter' which changed the face of the un position and gave coherence to defensive shooting. The machine had wo telescopes, each manned by an bserver, one concerning himself with racking the target's course and the ther with observing the target height. The telescopes were kept on the arget by the observers rotating ranks, and these were connected to enerators emitting a current pro- ortional to the speed of tracking. So target speed and height were now lisplayed on dials, having been accur- tely measured. By setting in a re- istence equivalent to the shell's

time of flight an artificial answer came out which represented the 'Predicted' position of the target. This was now converted into a bear- ing, elevation and fuze length, and the data order to the gun. Provided the target flew straight, level and at a regular speed, and provided the mach- ine behaved itself, the shell stood a good chance of arriving in the general area of the target.

It was what happened at this point which appealed to most people. To study the records of the Munitions Invention Department, the Ordnance Board and the Patent Office for those years is an education; one is forced to the conclusion that every man, woman and child in the British Isles had invented a new kind of anti-aircraft projectile. Towards the end of 1915 the Secretary of the Ministry of Muni- tions – which had only been in exist- ence for a few months – informed the War Office that he had over 200 de- signs of anti-aircraft shell submitted by the public, and asked the War Office to provide the services of an 'expert artillerist' to review them. He added that he had a similar num- ber of ideas for shells to remove wire entanglements, and asked whether the army had any ideas on this.

The War Office replied that it, too, had desks full of designs, and pro- ceeded to categorise them: firstly, there were shells which contained bullets or segments joined together, which were to be expelled by an explosive charge and would then scythe their way through the air and anything else in the way. Then came shells filled with discs or boomer- angs, also expelled by explosives to fill the air with flying sub-missiles. Next were shells built in pieces, joined by wire, which would be blown apart to cut through targets like a Bolas. There were also shells built in pieces but unconnected, shells filled with lengths of chain, with loose rods, with chains having grappling hooks on the ends; and finally, the most com- mon contestant, shells with knife-like arms which would spring out during flight and carve their way through the target. All these had been proposed, and many of them tried, but the majority of inventors had little or no idea of the conditions to which the shell was subject when the gun fired, and so many of their designs were hopelessly impractical. The other point missed by most inventors was that their shells demanded a direct hit on the target – particularly the expanding-knife variety – and of course if this minor factor had been met, a house-brick would have been enough to bring down most of the aircraft of the day, without going to complicated lengths.

Some of the ideas were sound enough but they overlooked the fact that the whole apparatus had to be packed into a shell three inches in diameter and about a foot long. Once down to this size the chains and wires were so short and thin that they ceased to have any possible value. In the end shrapnel and high explosive shell remained the principal projectiles, with an incendiary shell for use against the hydrogen-filled Zeppelins. It is interesting to see that many of the ideas of 1915 have seen a revival in the Missile Era, now that the carrying vehicle is much larger, suffers less shock on launch, and the complicated gadgets can be made to a practical size and still fit inside the warhead.

Having got the guns and the ammunition and gathered the men, the last problem to be solved was locating the target. The village policeman and telephone system was still capable of producing results where the raid occurred in daylight, over England, and was undertaken by a Zeppelin, but in the Flanders battle zone it was inapplicable. Here German strafers could roar in over the trenches and be behind the lines in a few minutes, catching the gunners unaware. The most obvious attribute of the early aeroplane was the noise it made, though to a generation accustomed to the jet engine the noise of a Mer-

cedes or a Gnôme-Rhône aero engine of 1915 is a lullaby indeed. So the basic system of detecting attacking aeroplanes was to listen for them; firstly by planting soldiers in open space and giving them phones to call back and warn the guns, later by developing sound detectors. These took two forms, large megaphone-like horns with a stethoscope earpiece at the small end, or paraboloid mirror with microphones at the focal point. Both were capable of hearing an oncoming aircraft long before the unaided ear, the French paraboloi

model having a range of fifteen kilometers in still weather. This model
also had the virtue of being highly
directional, and thus a rough estimate
of direction and height could be made.
The horn model simply told the listen-
er that something was coming and
gave a very rough direction. It was
later improved by mounting horns in
pairs and using a stereo method in
which the noise from the right hand
horn went to the operator's right
ear, and that from the left horn to the
left ear. By swinging the apparatus
until the sounds were equal in each

**And when they got down low enough
you did not need artillery anyway**

ear a more accurate direction was
determined. A further improvement
was to mount another pair of horns in
the vertical plane and feed the output
to a second operator to get an estimate of elevation. In the end, these
primitive-seeming devices, in the
hands of skilled operators, could de-
tect an approaching aeroplane ten
or twelve kilometers away, and the
operators could make a surprisingly
accurate stab at what type it was,

how fast it was moving, its direction and height, all of which enabled the gunners to be altered.

At night, since the gun relied on optical aiming, it became vital to illuminate the target, and for this purpose searchlights were developed. Linked with sound-detectors, once the sound team had found the target and indicated that it was within range, the light would be exposed on the bearing and elevation found by sound, and, it was hoped, would illuminate the aeroplane. If not, a short sweeping search should do the trick. Once the sound-guided light latched on to the target, two others would expose and join in, and once the trio had the plane in their grip, it took a smart aviator to shake them off. And, of course once illuminated, the guns could open up.

But suppose the cloud was low, visibility poor, the lights unable to pick up the target? Or the wind howling or the distant noises of railway trains or battle interfering with the sound locators, so that the aeroplanes were close in before they were detected? It is instructive to consider some figures here. Assuming the aeroplane was travelling at one hundred miles per hour, and the sound was detected when it was 6,000 yards away. Sound travels about 360 yards a second, so it would take the aeroplane noise sixteen seconds to reach the locator; and in that time the aeroplane had flown 800 yards towards him. In other words when the locator heard the noise of a target 6,000 yards away, it was actually only 5,200 yards away. Now allow thirty seconds for the locators to alert the guns, the gunners to take post, set fuzes, load and fire. By this time the plane is only 3,700 yards away. Having fired, the shell will take, say, twenty seconds to get up to the plane's postion. Where is the target by now? 1,000 yards closer, 1,000 yards this side of the shell burst.

All these facts were understood and corrected for when firing, but when the warning was scant, it is plain that the target could be past the guns before they had time to work out all the data. So for cases of this nature, the Barrage was developed, in which ranges and fuze lengths for each gun in a defensive area were so calculated that when all fired at once, an area of sky was studded with bursting shells and covered in flying fragments effectively making a lethal screen through which the target must fly or over which he would have to climb. Either way the guns were winning for it must not be overlooked that

the task of the anti-aircraft gun was not solely to shoot down aircraft; he was earning his living if the enemy aircraft was made to fly so high that he couldn't see to bomb or reconnoitre or photograph.

In the face of all these technical obstacles, it seems little short of miraculous if the gunner ever hit anything at all, yet in defiance of the mathematical odds some surprising results were obtained. Consider the number of aircraft destroyed by US Army anti-aircraft gunners in France.

Counting all the US batteries in action, one German aircraft was brought down for every 1,050 shells fired. If you count only the batteries which actually obtained hits, the figure comes down to one bird for every 604 shots. Indeed, one battery held the astounding record of bringing two aircraft down with its first 120 shots fired in France. It makes the mathematics look ridiculous.

A 13-pounder, weighing 9cwt, on a mark 3 motor lorry mounting

The price of liberty

On 4th August 1914 the Field Artillery Branch of the US Regular Army consisted of six regiments scattered throughout the Western Hemisphere; in the continental US itself there were two field regiments and half a regiment of mountain guns. The total strength was 266 officers and 4,992 enlisted men.

On 11th November 1918 the picture was somewhat different; 22,393 officers and 439,760 enlisted men manned sixty-one brigades of artillery, of which forty-two were in France, in combat or preparing for it. Added to these brigades were sixty-eight ammunition trains and sixty-one trench mortar batteries, plus numerous training establishments. The intervening years between these dates though had not been wisely spent. The bare figures given above would lead one to suppose that the increase had been gradual over the years from 1914, but in fact very little was done for almost three years. a circumstance

which made the battle infinitely harder when it finally had to be fought. To quote one set of figures, the April 1917 return of strength in field artillery personnel was 1,130 officers and 21,874 enlisted men, including National Guard and Reserve troops, an increase over the 1914 figure which is but 3.7% of the eventual increase. To put it another way, 96.3% of the increase took place in the nineteen months of US participation in the war, while the previous thirty-three months had been virtually wasted.

The reason for this disproportion lies, of course, in the political climate of neutrality which occupied the US during the earlier part of the war. While the professional soldiers were avidly amassing what information on battle technique that they could, and were under few illusions as to the final course of events, the publicly-acclaimed policy of avoiding entanglements in European affairs made sure that there were few recruits offering their services and little money available to provide equipment. The Mexican Border Expedition of 1914–15 had been a useful limbering-up exercise which, considered side by side with the reports from Europe, enabled reforms and doctrines to be planned ahead; but implementing those reforms in terms of troops and hardware was a different matter entirely.

In 1914 the US artillery consisted of two branches – the Field Artillery or 'Redlegs', and the Coast Artillery, or 'Cosmoliners'. The former derived their nickname from the stripes on their breeches, while the latter derived theirs from cosmoline, the tenacious greasy preservative compound liberally slathered on coast guns to protect them from the ravages of sea and spray. The field gunners were armed with the 3-inch Model of 1903, a serviceable and sound weapon, basically the Erhardt which the

US field artillery camped in Mexico in 1916; an expedition which acted as a useful training ground

British adopted under the name of 15-pounder, with a hydro-spring recoil system and a pole trail. About 600 of these were in stock in 1917. In 1913 work had begun on designing a new equipment to replace the 1903; this was to have a split trail, such as had recently been developed in Italy. This design gives considerable advantages to a field gun, since it permits greater elevation and traverse without having to move the whole carriage bodily. A pole trail gun is limited in elevation by the fact that the breech will strike the trail at a relatively low angle of elevation – sixteen degrees in the case of the M1903. Traverse is also limited by mechanical considerations, and, more important, considerations of stability: once the gun is aligned across the line of the trail, the recoil force tends to upset it and the gun is liable to roll over when fired. The M1903 gun had only four degrees of traverse on each side of zero. Over and above these mechanical drawbacks, the range of the M1903 was felt to be too short *vis à vis* its contemporaries, being 6,500 yards with the standard shrapnel shell. By adopting a split trail it should be possible to reach an elevation of forty degrees, giving a considerable increase in range, and have an arc of traverse of thirty or forty degrees each side of zero.

Lest it should be asked why anybody ever bothered to make any other kind of trail once the split type had been developed, it might be said that there are some disadvantages too, particularly where horse-drawn guns were concerned. The principal one is the necessity, for reasons of stability, for a split trail when folded together to be longer than a pole trail, and this of course adds weight behind the team and reduces manoeuvrability. In later years, when the gasoline engine became the prime artillery mover, this objection lost its validity and anything other than a split trail became a rarity in US service.

The medium gun of the time was the 4.7-inch Model 1906; this was quite an

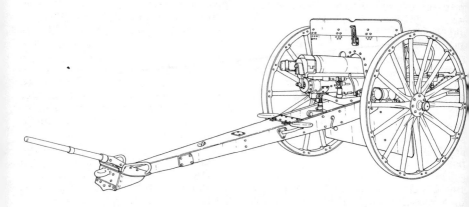

US 3-inch Field Gun M1903 based, like the British 15-pounder, on an Erhardt design, this US Army gun is typical of its era. The solid trail restricted elevation to 16 degrees and thus the range was only 6500 yards

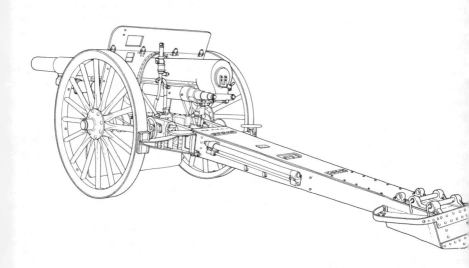

US 4.7-inch gun M1906. This was the standard medium gun of the US Army, but few had been made prior to entry into the war. Re-design to accept French 120mm ammunition held up production still further, and the gun's undoubted potential was never fully realised in action

efficient gun whose only shortcoming was insufficient range, though this was improved by adopting a 45lb shell in place of the original 60lb, a move which improved the range from 8,000 yards to 9,700 yards. This shell was later redesigned to a streamlined form which increased the maximum range to 11,000 yards, a procedure, which if anything were needed, should have finally convinced sceptics of the advantages of good ammunition design. But only sixty had been made between its introduction and the outbreak of war in 1917.

The mountain gun was a British Vickers design, the 2.95-inch or 75mm. This was a pack-artillery gun, designed to be broken down and slung aboard mules. There were only a few of these in service, but this design seems to have lingered on longer than any other weapon in American service. Introduced about the turn of the century, by 1917 it was obsolescent, and a publication of that year records that it was to be replaced by another weapon. But in spite of this it soldiered on, being used finally in the Phillipines in 1944 and 1945, although by this time it was ignored in every catalogue and publication dealing with artillery. I am not at all sure it's dead yet, or if it is, I doubt if it will lie quiet.

The Coast Artillery were liberally provided with weapons of every conceivable calibre, from 1.5-inch 3-pounders to 14-inch monsters firing three-quarter ton shells. But all these were firmly set in concrete in batteries and forts from Nantucket to Subic Bay, via Guantanamo and Panama, and the Cosmoliners were little concerned with the prospect of a European war. It was unlikely that any belligerent would try an assault on the USA, and nobody was suggesting that Fort Monroe should be dug out and sailed across to Europe.

So the situation on 6th April 1917 was that the US Army could deploy for combat some 660 serviceable field guns, with 275 officers and 5,233 men who were considered sufficiently trained to man

them. As far as heavier weapons were concerned, there were a few 3.8-inch, 4.7-inch and 6-inch howitzers of doubtful utility for which only a negligible amount of ammunition was in stock. All in all, not a suitable strength with which to wage war on the scale which was by then the accepted European norm. The only consolation was that there was an equally small force of other arms, so that at least the artillery would have the same breathing space as the rest of them, and the supporting gunners could be trained at the same time, and in concert with, the infantry and cavalry. But this training and equipping was to be a headache of the first magnitude.

One of the more pernicious doctrines which bedevils professional soldiers is the childlike faith of the legislators that all draftees are created equal. They are not. A draftee may make an outstanding cavalryman or signaller but a totally incompetent gunner or engineer; it's hard to quantify this, it just happens that way, and the US drafts of 1917 followed the pattern. Moreover, demands for such sophisticated trades as signallers, motor mechanics, specialists of one sort and another, creamed off the best men and threw back the dross to be divided between the combat arms, on the principle that any fool can be taught to carry a rifle, ride a horse, or shoot off a cannon. The result was a vast influx of unsuitable and untrainable men into the field artillery, and it took a great deal of time spent arguing at Chief of Staff level before the truth was driven home and a reasonable proportion of the more intelligent draftees allotted to the guns.

Once they were gunners, they had to be trained. Since the early days of the war, both the British and French armies had had military missions in the USA, principally to oversee military contracts but also to disseminate information to their US counterparts. The artillery sections of these missions immediately placed their knowledge and experience at the disposal

The Utah Light Battery in the Philippines, 1899. This campaign was the finishing school for many of the US Commanders of the First World War

of the US artillery, but the methods of imparting this information varied. The British Mission's artillery section was headed by Major-General Sir John Headlam, a distinguished gunner and future historian of the Regiment, and this group freely passed over information, training aids, recommendations and advice, and left the recipients to use it as they saw fit. The French Artillery Section, under Colonel Rielle, had some seventy-five officers dispersed over every field artillery camp in the USA, and these officers took it upon themselves to take charge of US training, indoctrinating them with what the French thought best. And therein lay the root of the US Field Artillery's problems for years to come. A large number of the US brigade commanders had no knowledge of artillery, and, finding themselves presented with one or two French experts who appeared ready and willing to assume the burden, they gladly turned over to them the responsibility for overseeing training in their brigades and accepted them as their artillery advisers. From then on only French systems were taught, only French equipment considered worthy of mention; anything else was decried. Compounding the mischief was the fact that there was, at that time, no Chief of Field Artillery, no one man with sufficient seniority to represent the field gunners at the highest level, integrate training, make decisions, programme equipment demands or formulate policy. Eventually such a post was formed, but it had little effect until the appointment of General William J Snow early in 1918.

Snow was firmly of the opinion that the static warfare of the Western Front would eventually come unstuck, once the weight of the AEF was ap-

plied, and that the more conventional mobile warfare would take over. He therefore laid down that training was to be along conventional lines, based on the simple principles of fire and movement, and that any modifications to suit trench warfare conditions could be learned later, when the basic ABC had been mastered. This was a wise policy but with it he came into collision with the French Mission, who wanted the US artillery trained simply as battering rams to support the next French advance. Matters came to a head in 1918 when a French officer arrived unheralded at the School of Fire, Fort Sill and proceeded to reorganise the system of instruction. The Commandant of the School immediately contacted General Snow, asking him to get the offender 'out of his hair' and Snow, in turn, had the errant missionary recalled to Washington.

The next problem with the French Mission came when Snow had only three trained artillery regiments in the US – the demonstration staffs at Fort Sill. He relied on these units to give the final training to the entire replacement strength of the AEF Artillery, and he was less than pleased to find that the French Ambassador, primed by the Mission, had requested President Wilson to send these three regiments to France forthwith. Wilson, appreciating that three regiments were unlikely to affect the outcome in Europe, declined.

Eventually, in August 1918, Snow had had enough; he went to General Peyton C March, then Chief of Staff, and asked him to get all the French 'helpers' out of the US as fast as possible. March agreed, but diplomacy demanded a gentle touch, and when the Armistice came there were several missionaries still in office, still causing friction.

But it is in the weapon procurement field that the most amazing tale unfolds. In 1914 the munitions industry in the USA was small and specialised. One or two companies – Bethlehem

Steel, Driggs-Seabury, Semple – made weapons and ammunition speculatively for international sale or on contract for the US Army or Navy from time to time. When the British and French purchasing missions began ordering munitions, these companies, and others, accepted contracts and began building weapons and making ammunition, thus amassing considerable expertise and the necessary machines, tools and work-force. Consequently, it might have been expected that the supply of weapons to the US Army in 1917 would have presented little problem. Nothing could be further from the truth.

When the US entered the war it was agreed that the simplest and quickest solution would be for General Pershing's AEF to be supplied with weapons from French and British sources, a course of action which would leave shipping free to ferry the maximum number of troops across the Atlantic. The British supply was largely in the trench mortar and heavy gun field, and the field artillery was to be entirely supplied by France, which tied the US artillery inseparably to the 75mm Model 1897, its associated ammunition, stores, fire control instruments, and, by inference, tactics. Once this agreement was made, the first step was to stop production of the American 3-inch M1903 and to start producing a weapon which would accept French ammunition. (Why nobody solved the problem by simply rechambering the 3-inch as it stood has never been satisfactorily answered; one can only assume that the objections to the M1903 – lack of range, limited elevation, pole trail and so forth which we have already seen, were sufficient to get it excluded from consideration.) Consequently, a most confused programme of gun construction and procurement was spawned.

The first weapon to be considered

General Pershing, during the Mexican expedition

as the new field gun was the improved 3-inch, the one with the split trail and sundry other modifications which had appeared from time to time and which had all been grafted into the improved design. This weapon was by now graced with a title – the Model of 1916 – and somebody had sufficient faith in it to order it into production forthwith. Now at this time procurement, development, design, specification, everything except actually shooting the guns, was out of the artillery's hands and firmly under the control of the Ordnance Corps. A Board of Ordnance and Fortification met and drew up requirements and made recommendations, but these were subject to the approval of General Crozier, Chief of Ordnance, and he had made his views plain as far back as 1901 when he flatly stated that he would have '. . . the testing of field guns conducted by the Ordnance Department, through the instrumentality of Ordnance Officers, by the methods of the Ordnance Depart-

ment, and at the Ordnance Department's place.' No amount of argument would move him from his viewpoint, and consequently the matter of decision on guns was kept out of the artillery's hands. The Model of 1916 was an Ordnance Department design; so in 1916 the Ordnance Department gave an order for 300 carriages, and in May 1917 a further 340 were ordered. June 1917 saw the New York Air Brake Company awarded a contract for another 400, and in December the Willys Overland Company were instructed to make no less than 2,927 carriages. It must be stressed that these orders were for carriages – that is to say the trail and wheels, elevating and traversing gear, and, most important of all, the recoil

One of the first French 75s to reach Fort Sill, this shows the position of the brake shoes during firing, to make the carriage more steady, and also shows the fuze setter on the front of the shield

**Loading limbers at an ammunition
supply point in France, 1918**

system. The gun to fit atop these
carriages was little changed from the
M1903 pattern, and presented relatively few problems to the gun-
making factories. In June 1917 the
gun was modified to take French
75mm ammunition, and from then on
one can suppose that production of
guns gave little trouble. But the carriage programme was running into
difficulties. An estimated 4,000 carriages had now been ordered, but no
one had seen them. In March 1918 –
two years after the first contract had
been given – the first carriage was
delivered. By the middle of 1918,
nineteen had appeared. By December
– when the war was over – 249 had been
delivered, and instead of the 'Model of
1916' it was being openly referred to as
the 'Crime of 1916'.

Why had the manufacturing resources of the USA failed so abys-
mally? For two reasons. Firstly, in an

endeavour to improve and improve,
to finish with the best possible gun,
scarcely a week went by without a new
drawing of some component arriving
on the desks of the harassed manufacturers; at no time did a competent
authority bang on the table and call a
halt to the unending stream of corrections and modifications, so that no
sooner did a contractor get a machine
set up or a production line running,
than he had to tear it down and start
again from a fresh set of drawings.

Secondly, and worst of all, it was a
basically bad design, once described
as 'an abomination' and as 'an impossibility as a practical manufacturing proposition'. One of the special
features of the gun was its ability to
fire at high angles, due to the split
trail, but the spring recuperator as
originally designed was insufficiently
powerful to return the gun to battery
after recoil at high angle firing. After
many attempts to correct this defect,
a hydro-pneumatic recoil system was
held to be the probable solution, and

the French designer who had developed the recoil system of the 75mm M1897 was contracted with to produce a similar system for the M1916. This he duly did, urged on at his drawing board by a fee reputed to be in the region of $60,000, and the result was known as the St Chamond recuperator. This led to more ill-feeling from the French government, who accused the US of 'stealing military secrets' but this teacup tempest soon died out. Meanwhile the one and only M1916 gun was ordered to France to be fitted with the new recuperator; *en route* it was 'lost' for several weeks, and was finally found at Halifax NS, where it had been dumped on the dockside for no particularly good reason. Eventually it arrived in France and the recuperator was fitted, and it was then shipped to a US Ordnance test establishment in France to be fired. The recuperator withstood the test firings satisfactorily, but on the sub-

sequent road and cross-country mobility trials the rest of the carriage fell to pieces. Moreover, the degree of slop and backlash in the training gears led to incredible inaccuracy in firing, and the prospect of using such a weapon to fire over the heads of friendly troops in battle was unthinkable.

Enough. The M1916 was a bad design, but it was persisted with in the fond hope that the US Field Artillery would eventually go to war with a US designed and built gun. This was a laudable motive in its way, but in the circumstances prevailing at the time, it was the wrong horse to back.

The second contender for the post of official cannon was one of impeccable background and proven worth –

The 155mm Schneider gun being brought into action ; numbers of these were provided to US units, but the design was not standardized in US service

Above : The British 18-pounder ; when rebarrelled to accept French 75mm ammunition, this became known as the US 75mm Gun M1917. *Below :* A couple of British visitors inspect a 75mm M 1897

the British 18-pounder. The Bethlehem Steel Corporation had made large numbers of these on British contracts since 1914, and so, on US entry into the war, the Ordnance Department gave Bethlehem another contract to make 268 of them for the US Army, chambering and rifling them to suit the US 3-inch ammunition. The following month saw the decision to standardise upon French 75mm *matériel*, so the designs were amended to accept 75mm ammunition, and, of course, production was held up while these changes were incorporated. But by January 1918 they were coming off the production line, a trickle at first, increasing if not into a flood at least to a steady flow so that by the middle of 1918 over 300 were available to units for training purposes, and contracts for another 1,000 had been given.

This gun – which became known as the 75mm Model of 1917, or 'British 75' – had a good deal of prejudice to overcome. It had a spring recuperator, and this was by now considered to be very old-fashioned; after all the old M1897 and the new M1916 used hydro-pneumatic recuperators. And there were all sorts of tales from France about the British battlefields being knee-deep in broken springs. Then too, it was a wire-wound gun: the inner tube of the gun was tightly wound with miles and miles of steel wire under tension before being enclosed in the outer tube. For some reason this system of manufacture was never held in much esteem by American experts.

In the event, however, the M1917 gave a good account of itself in its training role, and those who came to scoff remained to cheer, for once the troops actually got their hands on one and fired it, the prejudices soon disappeared. By the time the war ended it was so highly regarded that it was proposed to give contracts for a further 1,500 guns in order to be able to provide the weapons demanded by Pershing for the proposed 1919 offensive; but within a month of this decision being taken, the war was over

and the contract was never placed.

And so we come to the third potential US field gun – the French 75mm Model 1897. This entered service with the Americans by virtue of the French agreement to supply them to Pershing's AEF in order to save shipping space, and 1,828 of them were purchased for use in France. Sixty of these were then shipped back to the continental US for training use. The adoption of this gun was originally intended as a temporary measure for use by AEF until the supply of M1916s got under way to replace them, but as we now know the M1916 never did get under way. By the end of 1917 it was obvious that the M1916 was a non-starter, and a proposal was put up to cancel a contract with Willys Overland for some 3,000 M1916s and replace it with one for the same number of M1897s. The carriages were to be made without recoil systems; for it was the recoil system of the French 75 which presented the most problems.

The French 75mm M1897 was, as we have seen, the first successful quick-firing gun, equipped with a hydro-pneumatic recoil system, and it was virtually a state secret. The recoil system was the pride and joy of Puteaux Arsenal and the thought of actually having to divulge what went on inside it sent shivers up and down many a Gallic spine. In 1917 an officer of the US Ordnance Corps went to Puteaux Arsenal to learn the construction and maintenance of the system, and, in the process, he was heavily indoctrinated in the need for secrecy. Early in 1918 he returned to Washington with drawings and special tools and jigs needed to assemble and maintain the mechanism. No sooner had he arrived back than he locked everything in his desk and took off for a month's leave. During this time the existence of the drawings became known, but it took a lot of high-level pressure before the secrecy was overcome and the drawings taken out and made available for study by the people who were going to have to make them. At last, some contracts could be put out, and as a sop to secrecy, one vital component was split into minor sub-assemblies and farmed out to different contractors so that no one company had a complete knowledge of the entire system.

However, the first large manufacturers invited to tender flatly refused to do so. On hearing of this, the French Mission openly observed that they doubted whether any American company was capable of making the recoil system. Eventually, Rock Island Arsenal, feeling that the gage had been flung at their feet by that remark, said that they were prepared to try, and backed their opinion by promising delivery of 1,750 systems by January 1919. The Singer Company then took up the challenge and took on a contract for 2,500 systems. Indeed, one company, the New York Air Brake Company, actually demanded a contract, but as much as anything else, this was simply to get rid of the M1916 contract and do something useful for a change. By the nature of their normal products they were ideally suited to making such a device, but, like the Ancient Mariner's albatross, the M1916 was firmly hung around their necks, and nothing they could do seemed able to shake it off.

At about this time, in early 1918, fate took a hand. Yale University had, by some unrecorded process, obtained four worn-out M1897s from France and intended using them for training their ROTC members. What they lacked was a drill-book to tell them who did what, and a faculty member wrote to the Chief of Field Artillery to ask for one. The reply he got was unexpected; an offer to give him four new M1917s in exchange for the beat-up M1897s. He agreed, the exchange took place, the guns were removed, and one stripped and sent to Washington where, at long last, a French recoil system could be dismantled to see what was so secret that could not be seen on the drawings. And what was the secret? Fine tolerances, and an exceptionally close-fitting piston-head sealed with german-silver rings. Nothing more. It was simply a hand-built craftsman's job and one which was not likely to prove easy to make by mass-production methods, but beyond that there was nothing in that recoil system which was new or revolutionary.

Yet still the objections lingered. When one of the M1897s at Fort Sill succumbed to overwork it was dismantled to furnish instructional material and the recoil system was sectioned lengthways. A French officer there admitted it was the first time he had ever seen the inside of the system – and then went hot-foot to phone to call his Mission. They promptly pulled out all the stops, bombarding the Chief of Staff and anyone else who would listen with the accusation that the US artillery was disclosing French military secrets. It was no wonder that one US officer, sick of the whole business, went down in history by saying 'I guess the French would sooner lose the war than lose the secret of the 75.'

And what was the net result? Against all odds and the gloomy forecasts of various Cassandras, both Singer and Rock Island Arsenal eventually developed tools and assembly techniques which turned the Puteaux recoil system from a hand-built one-of-a-kind into an interchangeable mass-production component. But it took time; Rock Island's contract was signed in early April 1918 and they produced their first working system just before the Armistice. Singer's contract was a few days earlier but it was March

M1916s:	contracted – 5467	delivered by 11th November 1918 – 233
M1917s:	contracted – 1300	delivered by 11th November 1918 – 800
M1897 without recoil systems: 2927		delivered by 11th November 1918 – 50
M1897 recoil systems	3500	delivered by 11th November 1918 – 1

The German 77mm in action. The US 4.7in gun was seen as the answer to this weapon, but was not produced in sufficient numbers to affect the issue

919 before their first unit was ready.

Under the National Plan to equip a two-million-man army, 6,789 guns were needed. Allowing for the 1,828 guns bought in France and the 1,034 produced – and ignoring the fact that the 233 M1916s were unfit for combat use – there was a deficit, when the war ended, of 3,936 field guns. Furthermore, this takes account only of first-line combat units, and ignores the demands of the multitude of training establishments which had sprung up.

The medium gun field was no better served than that of the field gun. The 4.7-inch M1906 was considered to be a valuable gun to have in combat since, on paper, it could outrange and outshoot the German 77mm. But only forty-eight of these ever arrived in France, so that their effect against the thousands of German 77s was negligible. There was no one thing which bedevilled the production of the 4.7-inch; but only 175 carriages had been completed by the war's end and even less gun barrels to go on them. An additional complication was that the ammunition was peculiar to it, and could not be purchased in Europe, so that every round had to be shipped across the Atlantic. In an attempt to alleviate this aspect of the problem, the gun was redesigned to take French 120mm ammunition, but all that this achieved was further delay in production and three completed 120mm guns by November 1918.

The various howitzers available in April 1917, the 3.8-inch, 4.7-inch and the 6-inch were, on the suggestion of the French Mission, dropped from the books and relegated to training, and the French 155mm howitzer and gun were both adopted. This was a sensible choice, since whatever design had been selected the guns would have had to be built, so few were the older weapons on hand. Contracts were let

101

Above : French 120mm gun ; to standardize supply, the US 4.7 gun was rebarrelled to take this gun's ammunition. *Below :* US 108th Field Artillery firing a 155mm howitzer during a gas attack, October 1918

British 8-inch howitzers in production in the USA

or 155mm guns, howitzers, carriages, limbers, and, of course, recoil systems. Tubes, carriages, limbers – no trouble. Recoil systems – trouble. The same story as for the M1897, a design so complex and tightly dimensioned as to be the despair of manufacturers. Finally the Dodge Brothers agreed to try. During the winter of 1917 they built a special $10,000,000 factory and on 1st July 1918, as promised, delivered the first recoil system for the 155mm howitzer. Then they spat on their hands, took on the problem of building the system for the 155mm gun and solved that one too. By November 1918 they had made 800 howitzer recoil systems and one gun system. But none of the complete weapons were actually assembled before the war ended, and the only 155mm guns and howitzers in the US were ones shipped back from France for training.

The British 8-inch howitzer was under construction by the Midvale Steel company on British contracts. Therefore the simplest solution was adopted for the supply of a heavy howitzer – they were told to go on making them, this time for the US army. But it was ten months before

the first one was delivered. Finally the French 240mm howitzer was also adopted. This was a relatively unproved design, one which had been scaled down from a 28cm model built for sale to Russia. The 240mm was little more than a paper exercise when the US first heard of it; the Schneider company then built one, it was inspected by a US mission in France and accepted, and the drawings were then sent to the USA to start production. Schneider's were most helpful, even sending technicians across the Atlantic to help get production started, but conversion of the drawings to suit US manufacturing methods took time, and peace intervened before the first howitzer was built. When it did finally arrive, it burst at the first shot it fired, a fate which befell many of its successors, and it was the late 1920s before these weapons could be considered serviceable for issue.

It is strange to observe, after this chapter of accidents, that the 75mm gun adopted was not really the pre-

103

Above: US First Army 155mm GPF guns open fire in October 1918. *Below:* French 40cm Railway Howitzer. A few of these were manned by US Coast Artillery gunners

ferred weapon at all. Before the entry of the US into the war, Colonel Charles P Summerall had been despatched to France by Secretary of War Newton Baker in order to study the artillery equipment in use there and make recommendations as to what weapon the US should re-equip itself with in order to be on a par with current thought. Summerall was emphatic that in his opinion the 75mm was too light a weapon, firing too weak a shell, and the US should forthwith design and build a 105mm weapon as the standard field piece. But his report was pigeon-holed and his opinion ignored, and the 75mm calibre was, as we have seen, adopted for convenience and political amity.

A month after the Armistice, Special Order 289-0 convened a Board of Officers, consisting of Brigadier-Generals Westervelt, Callan and Ennis; Colonels Dillard and Rennell, and Lieutenant-Colonels Capron and Boatwright 'to make a study of the armament, calibers and types of matériel, kinds and proportions of ammunition, and methods of transport to be assigned to a field army'. This 'Westervelt Board' or 'Caliber Board' acted well and promptly and submitted their report in May 1919. Among many other sound observations was this recommendation: 'A weapon of about 105mm caliber on a carriage permitting a vertical arc of fire from minus 5 degrees to plus 65 degrees and a horizontal arc of fire of 360 degrees . . . the projectile should weigh about thirty to thirty-five pounds and should include both shrapnel and shell. A maximum range of 12,000 yards will be satisfactory. Semi-fixed ammunition and zone charges should be used.' By this time the Ordnance Corps' stranglehold on design and development had been broken and the artillery were now allowed to have a say in what sort of gun they wanted. The new Chief of Ordnance had gone on record as saying that 'If the fighting men want elephants, we get them elephants' and a new era of co-operation in design began. The recommendation for a 105mm howitzer was accepted and it was placed in service – in 1941.

However there was more to the US artillery in France than the field artillery. The Cosmoliners, who had feared that they were going to be left out of the fight, were soon reassured on that score. It was deemed vital to provide heavy railway guns to support the Allied efforts in the field, and to try and obtain parity with the Germans in this respect. The production of railway guns had to be on simple lines, and the simplest answer seemed to be to withdraw guns from the harbour defences of the US. In this way no less than 743 guns, from 5-inch to 16-inch, were earmarked for extraction, and 460 railroad mountings ordered – to give a surplus of barrels over mountings so as to take care of the replacement problem. And the men to man these weapons were the Coast Gunners who were familiar with them; so the 'Oozle-finch', the Coast Artillery's mythical mascot, found itself in France.

The First Expeditionary Brigade of Coast Artillery troops was organised at Fort Adams, Rhode Island, in July and August 1917 and finished up at Mailly-le-Camp in late September. This force provided twelve gun companies intended to operate thirty-six 10-inch ex-coast guns on rail mounts, whenever they were ready. Until such time as they were supplied, French railway guns, of whatever calibre could be spared, were issued to them, and training began. In February 1918 these units were ready to go, and were sent to support the French Fourth Army in the Champagne area. The distinction of firing the first US railroad gun shot of the war fell to Sergeant Joseph Rhuska of Battery H, 53rd CAC, who pulled the lanyard at 1410 hours on 14th February 1918.

Eventually this small force was reinforced and expanded, and by the time of the Armistice ten regiments, plus supporting troops, were operating

Above : US artillery firing 155mm howitzers near Varennes. *Below :* Experimental US 14-inch naval gun on railroad mount, in action in October 1918. *Right :* British 9.2-inch howitzer of the type supplied to US units

135 Siege Battery firing 8-inch Mark 5 howitzers, May 1917

five 14-inch US guns, four 40cm French howitzers, two 34cm French guns, twelve 32cm French guns, twenty-four 24cm French guns and twenty-four 19cm French guns, all on railway mounts. These units had operated in support of the French from Compiègne to Belfort, and in October and November 1918 were concentrated in support of the US First and Second Armies in the attacks in the Verdun area.

With the enormous expansion of the entire artillery branch, and with field artillery fully stretched to man the divisional artillery alone, it became an obvious course of action to have coast gunners man all heavy artillery and anti-aircraft artillery as well as the railway guns. 8-inch and 9.2-inch howitzers were provided by the British and eight more

brigades were assembled in France and deployed. Twenty AA batteries, seven AA battalions, two trench mortar batteries and seven trench mortar battalions were also provided, and, including specialists and supporting troops, the Coast Artillery strength in France by the Armistice was 3,618 officers and 78,622 EM, while another 878 officers and 35,015 EM organised into nine brigades, five AA battalions, four trench mortar battalions, an artillery park and seven ammunition trains were in the US awaiting their orders for France. The Coast Artillery had started the war with 750 officers and 20,000 EM; on 11th November 1918 the troops in France, awaiting shipment in the US, and standing by their guns in various harbour defences in the US and its possessions, totalled 5,931 officers and 153,139 EM, an impressive rate of growth.

The middle years

The year 1916, according to General Falkenhayn, Chief of the German General Staff, was to be a Year of Decision. The to-ing and fro-ing of 1915 had achieved no conclusive results, and Falkenhayn made a peculiar *volte face* in justifying his confidence. The various battles of 1915, from Neuve Chapelle through Ypres and Champagne to Loos, had confirmed his opinion that frontal attack on a defended position was a waste of time and men, and he had been content to thin out his defences and let the Allies batter themselves against them while the main German effort took place in the east. Now, however, with a masterly dialectic, he began a series of arguments to convince the Kaiser, and himself, that what was needed to get the Western Front moving was no less than a frontal attack against a defended position. But the position was to be carefully selected; for his idea was to threaten a point of overwhelming strategic or patriotic importance to France, and then let the

Allies bleed themselves to death by feeding in more and more troops to defend it. He was not particularly interested in capturing the defended point; indeed it suited his book not to capture it, but to be always on the point of doing so, so that more and more defenders would be thrown into his killing ground.

The choice of target he narrowed down to two·points; Belfort or Verdun. Both had played a considerable role in French history, and their part in the Franco-Prussian War was still fresh in many minds. So movement against them would raise a great outcry and no French general who fancied his job would dare raise any objections to defending them. Belfort was strategically valuable, and Verdun lay in a salient which made it tactically a logical target. In fact Verdun's salient was the official explanation for many years after the war, before Falkenhayn's policy of attrition was fully appreciated.

For Verdun was eventually selected as the site of the Battle of Attrition. It was no easy target, but then Falkenhayn was not unduly worried about how difficult it would be to attack – it was the difficulty of defence which concerned him. Verdun was another Liège – a city surrounded by a ring of forts erected after the war of 1870 which, together with the Fortress of Toul, formed the principal defensive point of the French eastern frontier. The fate of Liège and Namur had shown that this form of defence was no longer inviolable, and General Sarrail, the Fortress Commander of the time, had caused a trench line and earthwork defences to be laid out well beyond the forts. His successor, Coutanceau, tried to interest his superiors in improvements, but he was dismissed for his trouble. The armament of the forts had been periodically raided to provide stopgap weapons in the middle of 1915, to the extent that many of the smaller works were completely denuded of guns. More or less the only weapons remaining were super-heavy positional and high angle guns which it was impractical to attempt to remove, since they were not intended for transportation and were insufficiently powerful to make useful railway weapons. A number of smaller turret guns were also left because of the physical impossibility of getting them out of their emplacements.

In all there were twenty forts plus numerous outworks surrounding Verdun, of which rather more than half were between the city and the German lines. The principal ones were Douaumont, Vaux, Souville, Tavannes and Moulainville in the outer line, with Belleville, St Michel and Belrupt on the second line. Although Liège seemed to have pointed out the futility of such defences, the Verdun forts were of much better quality and design. When the Germans inspected Liège after its capture, one engineer commented that in his opinion the

Fort Vaux, one of the principal defensive points around Verdun

111

Fort Douaumont, before and after. The first photograph was taken in December 1915, before the battle began. The second in September 1916, and illustrates the obliterating effect of millions of German shells

Belgians had been swindled by the contractors who built the forts, for the concrete was of poor quality. Such a criticism could not be levelled at Verdun; the concrete was of the best, it was eight to ten feet thick, and the forts had been well maintained over the years. In order to make any impression on them, Falkenhayn was going to need some good artillery.

In fact Falkenhayn was relying on artillery to a very great degree. His intention was to kill Frenchmen, not allow Germans to be killed, and his force was restricted to some 140,000 troops. So to back them up and put the cutting edge on his 'mincing machine' he demanded, and got, an excess of guns. The 42cm and 30.5cm victors of Liège were installed; a pair of 38cm

guns of the type used in the battleship *Bayern* were assembled on special rail mounts and moved down to be emplaced in concrete pits with huge steel turntables. These monsters, nicknamed 'Max E', fired a 750-kilogramme shell to 38,700 metres or a 400-kilogramme shell to 47,500 metres and were mobile versions of a number installed in turrets on the North Sea coastline. Altogether Falkenhayn mustered twenty-four super-heavy howitzers – Berthas and Emmas, two 'Max E's', 150 medium guns (105mm and 155mm calibres), 128 21cm howitzers, 266 medium howitzers (105 mm and 155mm calibres), 247 field guns (77mm and 90mm calibres) and about 600 trench mortars of various calibres.

At this stage it is necessary to point out one feature of the battle which makes it virtually unique; that is that the man in charge of it did not know what he was doing. This is a comment which mud-covered soldiers have levelled at their commanders ever since Joshua set his troops

113

Above: German 15cm howitzer in action, one of the hundreds of weapons deployed against Verdun
Below: 128 of these 21cm howitzers were arrayed against Verdun

German 105mm howitzer M 98/09

marching around Jericho, but for once it is true. Falkenhayn was intent upon attrition, but he knew that he could not sell such an idea to Crown Prince Wilhelm, the commander of the Fifth Army which was opposite Verdun and which would be the army to undertake the attack. Wilhelm was, and always had been, hellbent on capturing Verdun, to the extent of having had some of the 42cm howitzers moved in as long ago as October 1915 in order to 'do a Liège' – though without much success. He also had a plan to attack Verdun in a pincer movement, one which might well have succeeded but Falkenhayn scotched this on the grounds that he could not spare sufficient troops to guarantee success and anyway such an attack could well come unstuck due to fire from French defences in enfilade. Having disposed of that idea he now produced his own plans, sold them successfully to Wilhelm and his staff and left them to it. Wilhelm and the Fifth Army were out to blow their way through the defences and capture Verdun – they thought. In fact, Falkenhayn had every intention of sitting on his reserves to prevent Wilhelm's advancing too far, so that the French could be tempted into moving in and being decimated by the guns.

The preparations for the attack went on throughout January. Light railways were built to carry the 2,500,000 rounds of ammunition to the guns and masses of concrete and iron to build vast underground shelters or *stollen* in which the first assault troops were to live until the moment of attack. All the activity had to be concealed from the French, but in spite of tight security the French realised that something was happening over the way. But GQG refused to believe that an attack would come in that quarter and only at the last moment were two divisions sent to Verdun as reinforcements, with another two 'on call'. The Verdun defences thus totalled about six divisions and about 250 guns.

The attack was scheduled to begin on 12th February, but Verdun received an eleventh hour reprieve. On the 11th the weather broke, and alternate rain and snow lashed the area in the worst winter storms for years. Crown Prince Wilhelm was a sufficient realist to postpone the attack until such time as the weather had improved and the ground was firm. This delay was fortunate for the French, since the 12th was the day on which the two reinforcing divisions took up their positions, and an attack

115

Battery of 21 cm howitzers in action

One of the 38cm ex-naval 'Max E' railroad guns opens fire on Verdun

on the original schedule would have struck just as the change was being made, catching the defences in considerable disarray.

For nine days the Germans sat and cursed the weather, hoping the French would remain oblivious to the immense build-up. On the 19th the skies showed signs of improvement, and hasty orders went out, alerting the attacking troops and declaring the 21st to be D-Day. And at 0715 on the 21st the long-delayed storm broke over the French heads. Heralded by two shots from the 'Max E' guns aimed at Verdun itself, the entire German artillery opened up with a roar which was heard 100 miles away. The French front disappeared in a fountain of shell bursts; everything was swept away in the avalanche of steel and high explosive. Trenches caved in on their hapless occupants, communications were wrecked, dugouts stripped of cover, parapets blown flat, and everywhere flew the scything splinters of red-hot steel, cutting, dismembering, killing. It was hell and it continued unabated until midday, when it stopped as suddenly as it had begun.

The dazed defenders now clawed their way to what was left of their positions, took up their weapons and prepared to repulse the forthcoming assault. But no attack came. This was probably the first application of a trick which which was to be repeated many times in the First World War and revived in the Second World War. The attackers sat tight, while on the opposing side observers carefully noted every sign of movement. Soon their reports gave a good picture of what defences remained a threat to the attack and where there were sufficient defenders to cause trouble. And after a short time had elapsed – sufficient time to allow the observed defences to be plotted on a map, notified to the guns and the guns to lay – the bombardment began again.

man army. The typical 'Over-the-Top, in line, advance' attack of successive waves of troops would have stamped all over the remaining French defenders and the German army would have been in Verdun before nightfall. Yet it never happened, because the German commanders stuck rigidly to their orders. The orders were that the attack was to be spearheaded by small probing patrols, securing and reporting back before the main assault moved up. So although the road to Verdun was almost open, the small patrols duly went forth. The French, battered and bleeding, were not quite the negligible factor that they were supposed to be and sufficient remained alive and alert to hold up these penny-packet patrols and give them an impression of strength. The German advance – except in one small sector where the German commander stretched his orders and piled his reinforcing units in on the heels of his patrols – was checked, and Prince Wilhelm's hope of taking Verdun had gone. Falkenhayn was relieved; the attrition phase could now develop.

As well as the swamping of forward defences, the German guns aimed at the French artillery. The preceding weeks had been spent in pin-pointing every French gun position, and a proportion of the German artillery – largely the 150 medium guns – were carefully working their way through the lists. With this suppressive fire, lack of communication, blinded or dead observers, and no inkling of what lay across No-Man's Land, the French guns were virtually ineffective.

After the bombardment had continued for a few more hours it seemed unlikely that anything would be left alive to impede the assault, and at 1600 hours the guns finally stopped and the assault began. And this is one of the war's great examples of lost opportunity; the French had been battered unmercifully for almost nine hours with the most intense artillery bombardment ever fired, before or since. They were dazed, battered, and by all reckoning could be considered a negligible impediment to the Ger-

The subsequent phases of the Battle of Verdun need not be explored here in detail, since it became a long drawn out slogging match, with exactly the result that Falkenhayn had hoped - unit after unit was fed into the mill and ground down. The opposing artillery hammered each other's ground into a moonscape of shell holes, linked by mud and filled with water. Never have the gunners been so unpopular. The noise was constant - like living in a forge, according to many contestants - and as each side strove to outdo the other, the guns were jammed in wheel to wheel. The French, recovering from the initial shock, rapidly brought up all the artillery they could spare; within a month they had 744 75mm guns and 570 heavier guns. By July the heavy weapons had increased to 800, and by the end of the year there were 980 field and 1,318 heavy installed – one gun for every four metres of front.

**Sectioned German gas shells,
illustrating the variety of type used
against Verdun**

And the end of it all? The Crown Prince abandoned his hope of capturing Verdun, but Falkenhayn and his staff kept the battle going for their original purpose of attrition.

One of the ingredients of the bombardment which shattered Verdun's defenders was a proportion of poison gas shells. These were a German development, born much earlier in the war than is popularly supposed. The common answer to the question 'When was poison gas introduced?' is 'Ypres, April 1915.' In fact the correct date is much earlier, how early depending on what is meant by poison gas. According to postwar statements a lachrymatory irritant substance was packed around the balls in shrapnel shell and fired against British troops near Neuve Chapelle in late 1914, but it appears to have been ineffective, since the British made no comment on it.

Since shrapnel is ideally burst some thirty to fifty feet above the ground to allow the bullet pattern to develop, the irritant was probably too dispersed by the time it reached the ground level to be able to compete with all the other irritants which abound on the battlefield.

The development of the gas-filled shell began as a search to find a chemical substance which could be used as a substitute for high explosive. As we have already seen, the demand for warlike stores caught all the nations unprepared and the Germans entirely failed to mobilise their chemical industry to provide the necessary supply of explosive to fill the sudden output of shell bodies. The Kaiser Wilhelm Institute for the Advancement of Science in Berlin was approached with the problem, and made a number of experiments, but after a laboratory explosion killed a professor, enthusiasm waned. However, the seeds of 'chemical warfare' had been sown, and a Doctor von

Tappen of the Institute suggested putting xylyl bromide, a tear-inducing compound, into shells and bursting them in the enemy's area, thus incapacitating him while the advancing German troops – suitably protected, of course – closed with him and won the day. By the convenient channel of having a brother on the General Staff, von Tappen's suggestion was taken up, but the army was reluctant to place total reliance on such an unknown quantity, and finally produced a design of 15cm shell in which about half the explosive was replaced by a lead cylinder containing the xylyl bromide, or 'T-Stoff' as it was codenamed. This proved successful and the shells were first used in action at Bolimov, between Lodz and Warsaw in January 1915. The attack was part of Mackensen's eastward drive, but it was not a success, being beaten back by the Russians in the course of a week of bitter fighting. The gas shells were ineffective, principally because the intense cold prevented the substance from vaporising into gas, and although the Russians belatedly realised that gas had been used, they failed to make much of it, and the British and French were left unaware that the German army were experimenting with such substances.

The Ypres gas attacks in April 1915 were made by using gas cylinders in the trenches, from which chlorine was released to drift in a cloud over the Allied lines. This system obviously depended upon the wind for its success, and the prevailing wind in Flanders is usually from west to east, which gave the Allies the advantage in cloud gas warfare. So to offset this, development of gas projectiles began in earnest. A few minenwerfer and howitzer shells

Aerial view of a gas bombardment showing troops advancing behind the bursting shells

Above : German 15cm howitzer detachment stand easy for coffee and a smoke
Below : German *Nebeltruppen* aligning the German version of the Livens Projector

were produced and used in the latter half of 1915, but the tendency was still to use a large explosive charge in the shell, and it was the French, in their retaliation at Verdun, who pointed the way to the correct construction of gas shells by using designs in which the main filling was phosgene gas and there was just enough explosive to crack open the shell and release the chemical agent.

This method was immediately adopted by all nations, and the next problem was what to put in the shells. Many substances are lethal enough in a laboratory but not very effective when scattered in the open. Others are admirable in their effect but could not be filled into shell, either because their weight upset the ballistics or their chemistry made them incompatible with the metal. Chloropicrin was a common lachrymatory substance; phosgene and diphosgene the preferred lethal gases. Prussic acid gas was favoured by the French but it proved to be less effective than had been hoped and was soon abandoned. Germany pioneered the arsenical smokes under the code-name 'Blue Cross', and these were capable of penetrating the gas masks of the day. So the Germans began using barrages of mixed Blue Cross and Green Cross (phosgene) so that the Blue Cross, penetrating the mask, made the wearer so uncomfortably short of breath that he eventually removed it, thus exposing himself to the much more lethal phosgene fumes.

The most important method of delivery came in 1916 with the British invention of the Livens Projector. This was a simple steel tube of about ten inches diameter, buried in the ground with its muzzle protruding. A small guncotton propelling charge was placed in the bottom of the tube, and a 'Livens Drum' loaded on top. This was a metal drum about the size of a five-gallon oil drum with a small charge of exposive and a large filling of gas. Numbers of these weapons – hundreds in many cases – were buried behind the front-line trenches and the electric igniters of the propelling charges wired together. When the word was given, a generator was cranked and the entire battery of projectors fired their ungainly missiles. They were almost silent, merely revealing their discharge by a flash, and within a few seconds the drums crashed down into enemy territory and liberated their cargo.

One cheap and effective Livens drum was the equal of an 8-inch howitzer shell in capacity, and the effect of hundreds of these suddenly dropping into an infantry area was lethal. The Livens Projector was the gas delivery system *par excellence*, because the British had quickly realised something which it took the Germans a long time to appreciate: that the only way to succeed with a gas attack is to overpower the defence from the start. It is useless to fire odd rounds here and there. As much as possible should be concentrated on one spot, and the Livens could do this better than anything else. Their concentrations were so great that a single deep breath in the target area could be lethal.

An amusing byway of the chemical warfare scene of that time, and one which is typically British, is the selection of codes to disguise the substances in use. Chloropicrin was concealed by the initials PS to commemorate the fact that it was developed by chemists of Lever Brothers at Port Sunlight in Cheshire. Similarly, ethyl iodoacetate became SK because it was developed in South Kensington, London. A mixture of prussic acid gas and arsenious chloride became VN, since the supply of prussic acid gas came from a French factory at Vincennes; and phosgene was CC since the first supply came from the French factory at Collognes. The most obscure of all was mustard gas, called HS; it took me many years before I tracked this one down and found that it was due to mustard being a German innovation, and hence

123

(if you please) Hun Stuff.

The Hindenburg programme of munitions production planned in 1916 made provision for a much increased gas shell output, and also the perfection of mustard gas, probably the worst of the war gases of that time. For mustard did more than attack through the lungs; it burned the skin and attacked the bloodstream, and, in the eyes, blinded its victims permanently and painfully. Moreover it was a persistent and contaminating gas. If an area was shelled with mustard, the gas would lie about on the ground where it would be as dangerous to the attacker when he came into the area as to the defender. After experience with this aspect of the gas, the German army made it a rule never to shell an area with mustard within three days of an attack, and consequently British and French troops, while they reviled the stuff, bore mustard gas bombard-

German 77mm field gun in action in the Champagne sector

ments with equanimity, since they practically guaranteed that there would be no attack for three days.

The first mustard-filled shells were ready in July 1917 and were then used by the Germans just before the Third Battle of Ypres. It was a considerable surprise to the Allies and it was some time before they managed to develop a viable manufacturing system to make their own supply for retaliation. Indeed, the Germans were quite convinced that none of the Allies had the chemical capacity to make mustard gas and that they were relatively safe from it themselves. They had eleven months in which to enjoy this belief, for in June 1918 the French began firing mustard, followed in September by the British. Mustard gas is capable of being made by a number of different methods, and analysis can disclose which method has been used. When the French began using mustard, the Germans at first thought that they had managed to build up a small stock by emptying German dud and captured

The 21cm howitzer in action, showing stocks of the improved 1916 pattern shell

shells, but analysis showed, to their astonishment, that the Allies were making their own by a different process. German chemists investigated further and found that the Allied method was more economical than their own, and plans were being drawn up to convert German production to the Allied system when the Armistice supervened.

The war on the Eastern Front was pursued with the same relentlessness as that on the Western Front. But the strength of Russia was being sapped from within, so the German task became easier as time went on. In the early days, though, the fight was desperate, and many ideas subsequently used on the Western were born and raised on the Eastern Front. As we have already seen, gas was one such innovation. Another was the development of artillery tactics and handling by one Lieutenant-Colonel Bruchmuller, an unknown reservist

officer of artillery who had been recalled to duty on the staff. He turned out to be one of the most brilliant artillerymen of all time, with a superhuman ability to divine precisely how much punishment would be needed to make a given target capitulate or crack sufficiently to be taken. His tactics were so effective that the German soldiers nicknamed him *Durchbruchmuller* – a pun on the word *durchbruch* – breakthrough.

Bruchmuller's name first became prominent in March 1916 in connexion with a German counterattack. As the Battle of Verdun gained in fury and drew more Frenchmen into the mincing machine, the cry went up for the British and Russians to make a move – any move – which would force the Germans to withdraw troops from

Verdun and thus relieve the hard-pressed *poilus*. The British were busy making ready for their attack on the Somme; most of the troops were still in training, and any presumptive action would only jeopardise their plans for a major attack. The Russians were also making plans, but they agreed to mount a hasty attack on a limited front between Lakes Narotch and Wisniew in the hope of putting sufficient pressure on the German forces to panic them into pulling troops out of Verdun.

The attack failed completely; it scarcely breached the German line nor caused any hasty movement in the rear. In fact it was of so little consequence it is scarcely mentioned except in the most detailed official histories. Once the Russian attack had been held, the Germans, as was their wont, counterattacked, and the success of this was largely due to Bruchmuller's

Russian 76.2mm field gun in a defensive position

artillery. Whether or not he had the talent for divination ascribed to him, he certainly had a nose for likely targets and the flair to abandon set rules and vary his approach depending upon his target. He was quite capable of using a barrage here, a concentration there, gas and smoke elsewhere in the same attack, without worrying about what the book said. In the Narotch-Wisniew counterattack he used a series of short and sharp concentrations put down upon the expected rallying-points, HQs, gun positions, communications centres and supply dumps and lines which demoralised the Russians, and then switched to a quick rolling barrage which swept the Russian soldiers back to their original start line and beyond. Bruchmuller had arrived.

His big chance came in September 1917 when he was with General Hutier and was given the task of planning the artillery preparatory fire and support for the attack on Riga. The Russians, racked by revolution and debate, were

Russian 155mm howitzers of French parentage

now retreating. Riga, Queen of the Baltic, was a target the Germans had long coveted; in 1915 they had been repulsed in a bloody fight, and with the Russians in disorder it looked as if they might be allowed a second bite at the cherry. But the Russians and Letts holding Riga had other views on the matter, and the city was strongly defended by a series of well entrenched positions. Hutier's troops were numerically inferior to the defenders, and it was obvious that a straight attack would come to grief. Hutier therefore introduced a new tactic into the war, one which, in 1918, was to prove effective against the Allies on the Western Front – infiltration. Instead of throwing solid lines of men against the defences, small self-sufficient groups would move out, probe the defences, and then ease their way in where the line was weakest, fanning out to take troublesome redoubts in the rear. Bruch-

muller's task was to prepare the way.

The attack was to be made by three German divisions on a 9,000-metre front and included the task of crossing the River Dvina, 300 metres wide at that point. This was to be done initially in boats, pontoon bridges being thrown across later. The German bank of the river was well wooded, and allowed Bruchmuller to conceal 750 guns and 550 minenwerfers, split into two groups, IKA and AKA. IKA guns were for infantry support and were provided with ammunition in the proportion of four-fifths high explosive and one-fifth Blue and Green Cross gas. The AKA group guns were for counterbombardment of Russian artillery and HQ areas and used a proportion of a quarter HE to three-quarters gas.

Commencing at 0400 hours, all the

127

guns hammered as hard as they could go onto the Russian artillery positions, three batteries of 15cm howitzers being specially employed in seeking out command posts, communication points, observation posts and similar nerve-centres. At 0600 the AKA group continued with their counterbattery fire while the IKA group turned its fire onto the infantry positions defending the river. This bombardment continued until 0910 hours, shifting about the area, changing from explosive to gas and back again, all the time at hurricane intensity. At 0900 the AKA group joined in, each AKA battery leaving one gun to 'stoke' the gas clouds enveloping the Russian batteries while the other guns intensified the fire on the infantry.

At 0910 all the guns swung into a rolling barrage which dwelt on the forward Russian line until the assault boats were across the river, and then moved forward into the defensive zone. Behind it came Hutier's men, not in prolonged lines, but in small groups, probing, bypassing, enfilading.

The entire operation was a complete success and vindicated the theories of Bruchmuller and Hutier. The German casualties were few – largely, it seems, pioneers occupied in installing the pontoon bridges and thus presenting a relatively stationary target. The intense bombardment and concentration of gas totally unnerved the Russians, many of whom abandoned their positions and fled. Within twenty-four hours the Germans were firmly in control of Riga, and the Baltic was on the way to becoming a German lake.

Prior to this of course, Bruchmuller's touch had paved the way for many smaller attacks on the Eastern Front, but, together with Hutier, it was the Riga attack which brought him into prominence. Later in the year these two were called back to Germany and then despatched to the Western Front where their talent for getting through obstacles looked like being stretched to its utmost.

On the Western Front it was 'the mixture as before'. In an endeavour to take the pressure off the French, Haig brought his August attack on the Somme forward to 1st July. Much has been written about the Somme, and it can be briefly summed up: over 1,500 guns, 2,000,000 shells, eight days of bombardment by explosive and gas, followed by a monlithic infantry assault. Result: 60,000 casualties on the first day alone. The Allied tactics on the Western Front had degenerated to an arithmetical exercise which can be expounded like a Euclidian proposition: an attack, like Verdun or the Somme, on a single point, will develop a salient – a bulge in the line – and for a variety of reasons it can be shown that it will settle down roughly in the shape of a triangle with forty-five degree sides. In other words, the penetration will be about the same depth as the width of front of the attack. To determine how wide a front is needed for a particular attack is also reducible to mathematics: enough space must be ensured to leave a corridor in the middle of the salient so that troops passing up to the point are immune from fire from the flanks. If a fifteen-mile wide corridor is required, the front should be about twenty-five miles wide. In order to penetrate this, troops are needed in proportion to the defences; for every line of defence, one division.

One division had a front of about 1,500 yards, against the first line of defence, rising to about 3,000 yards against the third and fourth lines. This adds up to something like fifty-five divisions to do the initial attack on a twenty-five-mile front. Fresh divisions must be ready to move in to keep up the momentum of the attack, stepping up the total of men required to seventy-five divisions to push an attack five miles deep – at First World War figures, about 1,250,000 men.

General von Hutier, victor of Riga, and the man who put movement back into the battlefield

129

Above : British 8-inch howitzer gunners hard at work in 1917. *Below :* British 6-inch gun; ex-coast guns mounted on howitzer carriages, they rapidly became indispensable as long range support weapons

Once this horde has been committed in the salient they have to be fed, supplied with ammunition and stores, and the wounded evacuated. This is the rock on which this type of operation usually foundered and the reason why most of these attacks were unsuccessful. The other reason for their failure was the terrain that the soldiers had to fight across. Even if it was as level and well-manured as a polo ground before the battle, by the time the artillery had finished their preparatory fires, it was an obstacle in its own right.

The climax of what is termed the 'Pure Destruction' era of the artillery war was Third Ypres, or, as it is engraved on many a British heart, Passchendaele. This operation came in two parts, the first a limited attack on the Messines Ridge in June 1917, followed by what is variously known as the Battle of Flanders, or the Third Battle of Ypres or the Battle of Passchendaele in July – an attempt to push the German right flank back and clear the Belgian coast. The Messines battle was a simple move to pinch off a German salient and it was fought by General Plumer's British Second Army of twelve divisions against Sixt von Arnim's German Fourth Army of fourteen and a half divisions. Plumer, an astute soldier, had laid his plans well in advance, and Messines' greatest feature was the use of extensive underground mines, twenty of which were excavated and stuffed with explosives well before the battle. There was no surprise or finesse in the artillery preparation, which was simply an eleven-day hammering of every possible German position, with long range guns interdicting the approach roads and railways so as to prevent reinforcements being moved up. The Germans knew full well what was coming, but the surprise element of the attack lay in the mines. Mines themselves are, of course, as old as warfare, but nineteen of these enormous *fougasses* (one had been inadvertently destroyed by the Germans

before the battle) containing 600 tons of explosive, had such a shattering effect and altered the landscape so vastly that the German defenders were at a considerable disadvantage. Supported by tanks and a rolling barrage, the New Zealand and Australian troops took their objectives relatively easily. General Plumer is said to have observed on the eve of the battle: 'Gentlemen, we may not make history tomorrow, but we shall certainly change the geography.' By nightfall the objectives had been reached and with the help of massive artillery support Plumer's men stood off all counterattack attempts, secured their positions, and stayed put until 1918 when, with equal sagacity, Plumer abandoned the position and gave up his gains in the face of a desperate German attack.

So Messines was a success. But the following affair was a bloody shambles. One reason was geographical. Flanders is excellent country for defence, but a terrible locality in which to attack. In time of peace it is an agricultural area, low-lying, the water table close beneath the surface. In order to render the land suitable for tilling, the whole area was networked with drains and dykes to keep the water down. Artillery bombardment disrupting this system meant that the water, instead of draining away, rose, softened the ground, and quickly turned productive farmland into slippery bog. Add more bombardment to churn up the bog and you end up with a sticky morass which prevents movement; men and horses founder, machines bog down in the shell holes, and morale sinks. Add to this, as happened in July 1917, an outburst of highly unseasonable rain, and you have all the ingredients for a failed offensive.

The British army piled into Ypres the greatest concentration of guns ever seen in British history. 120,000 gunners manned 2,300 guns of every calibre. 321 400-ton trainloads of ammunition were shipped forward and shot off in a preliminary bombard-

German pilot's view of British tanks at Cambrai

ment which went on for nineteen days making a total of 4,283,000 shells to rip up the whole surface of the future battlefield and turn it into a bottomless morass in which the troops were sentenced to wallow for the better part of five months. It was into this scene that the German army introduced mustard gas, and the conditions were about as perfect as could be imagined, since the tenacious liquid settled on the mud and water and remained potent for days, being redistributed by every shell which burst.

By this time the tank had taken its place in the order of battle; indeed tanks were used at Third Ypres much against the better judgement of the Tank Corps, for the bog simply swallowed them up. It has been said that the only good thing to come out of that muddy struggle was that Hindenburg became firmly convinced that tanks were useless contrivances and consequently gave no encourage ment to those Germans who wanted to develop tanks of their own. But

during the advance.

These features were finally argued through and put to the test in the Battle of Cambrai. There were many innovations in this battle; tanks were going to be used in terrain of their own choosing; the utmost secrecy was observed; there was no long preliminary bombardment to alert the Germans; there was not even preliminary registration of targets, fire being brought to bear from map data; normal artillery activity continued right up to the moment of the attack so as to prevent German Intelligence from deducing new gun positions and from them assessing the probable course of future events. Lessons were learned from Riga and gas and smoke were used, partly to neutralise the German artillery and partly to help conceal the tanks. Seventy 60-pounders fired 16,000 rounds of gas at the hostile batteries, followed by 6-inch howitzers firing HE. A fast-moving barrage preceded the entrance of the tanks, and the ammunition allotment was one-third smoke, one-third shrapnel and one-third HE. This barrage was laid 300 yards ahead of the tanks, and instead of advancing by nominal 100-yard stages, it leaped from trench line to trench line; no longer did the barrage have to sweep each yard of the terrain, since the machine gunner in the shell hole could now be dealt with by the tanks. Several separate smoke screens were also fired during the advance in order to mask the activity of the tanks from various possible observation areas, while the whole attack was supported by heavy guns and howitzers firing concentrations on to any likely point of activity. Finally, a number of long range guns were brought up to deliver harassing fire on the German rear.

A number of vital lessons came out of Cambrai, not only for the tank men but for the gunners too, and as 1918 was just around the corner, they were carefully studied for incorporation into the next year's offensives.

ninking men – and there were some – bserved that in the tank they had a evice which could take two tasks off he shoulders of the artillery. The ank could crush wire obstacles, so no ong, destructive bombardment was eeded; and the tank as a weapons atform could give direct fire support o the infantry until they were dug in nd capable of using their own eapons. Hence, long bombardment nd close barrage could be dispensed ith in favour of short bombardments great intensity together with more ppressive fire on to specific localities

The last efforts

The German spring offensive in March 1918 was not entirely a surprise to the Allies, in that they were aware that something of the sort was bound to happen. The French High Command had, moreover, learned from sundry sources that the Germans had a surprise up their sleeve in connexion with this attack, though the precise nature of the surprise was not known. At 0715 hours on 23rd March 1918 – two days after the offensive against the British Fifth Army had begun – the surprise was unveiled. There was an explosion on the Quai de Seine, in the 19th Arrondissement of Paris, loud enough to be heard over most of the city. While speculation was still rife, fifteen minutes later came a second explosion, this time closer to the centre on the rue Charles V. Then after another fifteen minutes pause, a third explosion on the Boulevard de Strasbourg, near the Gare de l'Est.

The obvious reaction was to assume that Paris, which had been bombed

before, was now under another bombing attack, this time from some new machine which flew so high as to be invisible and unheard to the ground observers. But the explosions continued to shake the city at uniform fifteen-minute intervals, until twenty-one incidents had occurred. After the first three or four, business in Paris came to a standstill. Shops and offices closed, part of the Metro ceased to operate, many railway stations closed, and a goodly proportion of the population were out in the streets, craning their necks to try and be the first to spot the mystery raider.

Military experts had been called to the scenes of the first explosions, and by mid-morning they had picked up enough fragments around the points of burst to arrive at the startling conclusion that the mysterious explosions had been caused not by aerial bombs but by artillery projectiles. Paris was being shelled by an incredibly long range gun. Considering the German lines were the best part of sixty miles away, this was a very long range gun indeed, and the Heavy Artillery Section of the army was called in to get out their slide rules and comment on the feasibility of such a notion. After some figuring, they replied that such a performance would demand a gun with a muzzle velocity of about 4,500 feet per second and, while it had never been done, they saw no reason, given a long enough gun and a suitable propellant charge, why it should not work. And by the time the first day's bombardment came to an end, it was accepted that Paris was indeed being shelled by some giant gun located behind the German lines, possibly some 110 kilometres or more away.

The next morning's newspapers produced few theories of their own; one which was advanced was that the shells falling in Paris were actually carried within a much bigger shell

fired from some colossal mortar. At the vortex of its flight, this super-shell fired the smaller one out to give a much increased range; much the same idea as the multi-stage space rocket of today. Another theory was that in fact the gun was concealed in a wood or quarry or some similar deserted spot in French territory and much nearer to Paris. This attracted a great deal of support and search parties – some official, some not – took several days combing the more likely spots. A third theory was that the shells were silently launched from a pneumatic gun sited in Paris itself and operated by German agents.

The examination of the first day's shooting gave rise to some interesting questions. Nineteen shots had landed in the city itself and two on the outskirts. Fifteen people had died and thirty-six had been wounded. The craters – where shells had landed in open spaces – averaged fifteen feet in diameter and were five feet deep, and where shells had struck buildings it seemed that they penetrated for some distance before detonating. But the biggest puzzle was the plot of shell impacts. If the gun were near Paris, then what was it aimed at for each round? For none seemed to have landed close to any valuable target. On the other hand, if the dispersion of the shots were the natural dispersion of a gun at long range, then it must indeed be a very long range, and it must have so poor an accuracy as to make it worthless against any target much smaller than Paris. And finally, its mean point of impact was short of what one would expect it to be – the centre of the city. In fact, plotting showed the mean point to be about the Gare du Nord, in itself not a bad target.

On 24th March twenty-two shells fell, killing eleven and wounding thirty-four. On the 25th six shells fell, killing one and wounding three, and then the bombardment stopped. But this was only to be a brief pause, and on Good Friday, the 29th, the firing began again. This day was to be the

worst of the entire bombardment; of our shells fired that day only one fell within the city walls, but this passed through the roof of the Church of St Gervais and detonated against a supporting arch, knocking out the keystone and collapsing the entire roof on to the congregation. Eighty-eight were killed and sixty-eight wounded.

The bombardment fell into three phases; 23rd March to 1st May; 27th May to 11th June, and 15th July to 9th August. In all, 183 shells landed in the city and 120 outside, killing 256 people and wounding 620. After the first few days, business returned to normal, and the bombardment was treated more as an irritation than a disaster. If the intention was property damage, it was a failure. And if the intention had been to demoralise the population of Paris, then it too was a failure; if anything, it made them more angry and determined than before.

After the first few days, too, sufficient data had been deduced from plotting the fall of shells and examining the orientation of holes in buildings to make a reasonably accurate assessment of where the 'supergun' was hidden. The location deduced was the Forest of Gobain, between Laon and Soissons, and aircraft were sent over to confirm this. A number of possible positions were spotted, though there was no sign of a gun, and a 340mm railway gun was brought up behind the French lines in order to work over the possible sites. To confuse German sound-ranging devices, two other guns of lesser calibre were sited nearby and when all was ready the smaller guns fired one or two seconds ahead of the 340mm. After a day of this bombardment the aeroplanes went over again and reported that one position had been destroyed and that the remaining positions, some of which were out of the gun's range, were now attacked by bombing planes and reported as

Professor Rausenberger, the genius behind the Paris Gun, Long Max, Big Bertha, and many other Krupp weapons

severely damaged. But for all this endeavour, the gun continued to fire as and when it liked, no damage having apparently been done to it, and it was not until an Allied advance overran the area that its operations ceased.

Not until the war was over did the details come to light, and then only reluctantly and after much digging by the Allies. The weapon seems to have been the brainchild of Professor Rausenberger of Krupp's, the man behind Big Bertha's development as well, aided by Engineer Eberhardt of the Vienna Military Academy. Seven guns of 21cm calibre were manufactured from worn-out 38cm naval guns. The 38cm was bored out and a 21cm inner tube inserted which projected for forty-two feet outside the 38cm body. Over this section a new jacket was shrunk and secured to the 38cm gun body. The inner tube was then rifled and the muzzle end shaped into a series of interrupted collars. On to these a smooth bore barrel extension six metres long was fitted, giving a grand barrel length of forty metres

Long Max, a 38cm railroad gun. It was this gun which formed the basis for the Paris gun

137

(130 feet) and a weight of almost 142 tons. Experimental firing with the first model on the German coast showed that a range of 132 kilometres (eighty-two miles) could be readily reached, since the shell spent most of its time in the stratosphere, and designs of cartridge and shell to achieve the best performance were soon prepared.

The carriage was of simple construction, based on naval design, with a large cradle within which the gun could recoil about five feet. This cradle was slung about massive trunnions in a box-girder erection of a railway mount of the type usually provided for the parent 38cm gun. At the firing site a massive foundation of concrete about fifteen feet deep was laid and upon this a turntable was built. This revolved on 112 eight-inch steel balls and was about twenty-eight feet in diameter. Railway track was laid up to and beyond this turntable, which carried a massive steel support. The gun was pushed across the turntable and centralised, then jacked up and the wheel trucks removed. Then the gun was jacked down until it mated with the support and turntable where it was secured by bolts against the firing shock.

One considerable problem was the supporting of such an enormous length of barrel, which was prone to droop from its own weight. This was corrected by a system of braces attached above the gun which supported the weight and gave the necessary alignment between muzzle and breech. In spite of this bracing the barrel vibrated when fired, flexing up to a meter above and below its correct alignment, an alarming display which usually lasted for a good minute after each shot was fired.

Another problem was concealing the huge weapon, and steel sockets were sunk all round the position, even between the railroad tracks, into which complete trees, sawn in distant parts of the forest, were erected and changed periodically as they wilted.

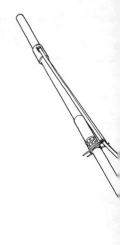

The Paris gun. This was a 38cm naval gun linered down to 21cm with an inner tube which projected beyond the parent gun and was extended by a six-metre smooth-bore tube. The resulting 130-foot barrel was heavily braced in order to counteract the droop due to the enormous weight and also to damp out the vibration due to firing. The carriage shown here is of the first pattern to be used over a concrete emplacement

The Paris Gun fires its proof round

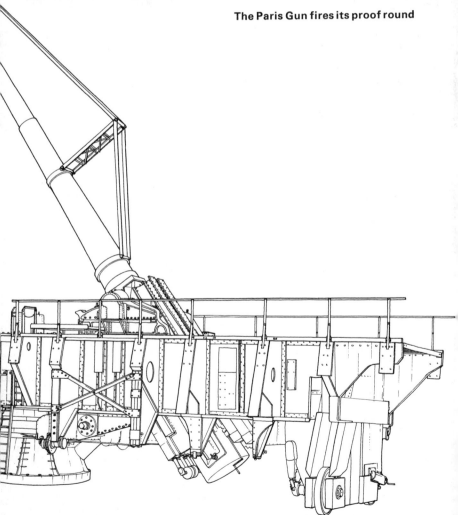

21cm Spgr. L/4,5 m.H.

Zusatzkartusche.

29,0

68,5

65,5

100 Kg

125 cm

100 cm

75 cm

50 cm

25 cm

M. G. 3 m.

A round of ammunition for the Paris Gun ; the shell, the adjustable portion of the charge, the base portion, and the cartridge case

Once all was in position, firing commenced. But with a gun like this there was rather more to firing it than pushing in a shell and a cartridge and pulling the string. The shell weighed 264 pounds, was 21cm calibre, had two copper rotating bands, and was splined externally to match the rifling, since the rotational force developed by the massive charge would have sheared the normal rotating bands. Each barrel was provided with sixty numbered shells, the diameter of which slightly increased as the numbers progressed. This was to counteract the inevitable wear of the gun due to the shell's friction and, more especially, to the heat generated by the explosion of the 400lb powder charge. After sixty shells the barrel, it was considered, would be too worn to shoot, and it was then to be withdrawn from the mounting and a

fresh barrel fitted in place. The old barrel was then returned to Krupp's to be bored out and rerifled, this time to 24cm calibre, and provided with a new outfit of projectiles.

When the first round had been fired, the second shell was rammed home and the distance of the ram carefully measured. Due to wear, the ram distance lengthened by a few inches at every shot, and thus the volume of the powder chamber increased. In order to shoot accurately, the muzzle velocity was to be consistently held to 5,000 feet per second, and a change in chamber volume would alter this figure considerably. At this sort of velocity and range a change of 100 feet per second in velocity could alter the range by a mile, so with the new chamber volume computed, a charge weight to suit was worked out, weighed, bagged, placed in the cartridge case, and brought quickly from the temperature-controlled powder car to the breech. The gun was then loaded, elevated to fifty-five degrees and fired. It was this long performance between shots which dictated the rate of fire at fifteen-minute intervals.

A difficulty which had been anticipated was the matter of discovering where the shells were actually falling, so that corrections could be made if the initial calculations had gone wrong and the shells were actually falling harmlessly in the countryside. A chain of agents was set up, and as soon as the Paris agent had been around the city and discovered details of the points of impact of the first few rounds he encoded them and passed them on by a telephone call to another agent near the Swiss frontier. A peasant crossed the border with a haycart. Someone telephoned to Basle. And within four hours of firing the first shot, the commander of the Paris Gun was plotting the impacts on his target map.

The last problem was to conceal the firings from the French sound-location system. This was done by bringing up thirty assorted batteries of all calibres and dispersing them around the area. Whenever the Paris Gun spoke, its tell-tale voice was drowned in a chorus of thirty batteries all firing at the same time.

From available records it seems that three mountings were built. The first gun fired on 23rd, 24th and 25th March and then went out of action to have a new barrel fitted, the rate of wear being higher than predicted. The second began on 29th March but fired only a few rounds. It is believed that this gun had a premature detonation in the barrel which wrecked it, due to loading a high-numbered shell out of sequence, but no official admission of this was ever made. Its task was taken over by the third gun. These two were rebarrelled twice in April. The final series of shots, from 15th July to the end, were fired using the 24cm replacement barrels, and a plot of these later shots displays evidence of considerably less accuracy and greater dispersion than with the original calibre.

When the Allies advanced in August, the Paris Guns (known to the Germans as the Kaiser Wilhelm Geschutz) were withdrawn. One platform fell into American hands near Château Thierry, fifty-five miles from Paris, but it appeared not to have been used and was probably for future employment, in order to bring the gun nearer to Paris and improve its accuracy. No guns were ever found. It can only be assumed they were cut up and scrapped as the end of the war approached, and their usefulness ended, but I well remember as a boy in the 'thirties being told by an old soldier that in fact they had been laid down in Krupp's scrapyard and covered with rubbish to escape the eye of the Allied Disarmament Commission. Which, I suppose, is just the sort of story that old soldiers tell to young boys. But it is remarkable that even today little has ever been admitted about the Paris Gun; German munitions workers in the postwar days, who spoke with complete freedom on every other aspect of munitions production, were curiously reluctant to talk about the Paris Gun. It may have been salted away for the future, but if so, it never showed up in the varied armoury of the German Reich in the Second World War.

The Paris Gun was the most glamorous gun of the First World War, seconded by the Big Berthas of Liège. But the other contestants had also been busy in their workshops since 1914, and by 1918 the weapons available covered every aspect of the gunner's arts.

After early efforts of the German howitzers at Liège the potential of heavy artillery was finally appreciated. There had never been any shortage of designers willing to put such monsters on paper, or manufacturers to build them – the difficulty lay in persuading the soldiers to try them, and that was the sticking point. As long ago as the Crimean War a British designer had produced plans for a 36-inch mortar to bombard Sebastopol, but it took a direct order from the Secretary of State for War before the

Above : Big guns are all very well— until you have to move them. *Below :* Heavy German gun at the moment of recoil. It is the absorbing of this force which demands gun carriages be made so strong and therefore heavy

army would accept it, and by the time it was ready the war was over. A few proof rounds were fired to keep up appearances, after which it was parked in a corner of Woolwich Arsenal and left to rust away. Public outcry and Parliamentary pressure forced the army to accept four 17.72-inch 100-ton muzzle-loading guns in 1880 in order to keep parity with the Italians who had bought some from the same maker. After five years of desultory use in proof ranges, two went to Gibraltar and two to Malta. They fired a few bedding-in rounds and then went to sleep; in fact they are still there. Similar stories can be told of American and French apathy towards monster designs, and it is not entirely the dead hand of reaction, but more of a skepticism of the whole problem of actually handling, serving and moving such heavy articles. For coast artillery the problem was alleviated by the introduction of power, first steam and then hydraulic, but with field weapons it all came back to horses and men. The internal combustion engine and the railway were the answers, but the railway was really a continental answer and the internal combustion engine relatively untried and untrusted. But Liège showed what was possible, and the big gun advocates were given their head.

Just before the war the British army had taken delivery of a 9.2-inch howitzer, and was giving it a leisurely trial before committing itself to the purchase of any more. When the war broke out, the howitzer was immediately shipped to France and more were ordered. This first weapon, christened 'Mother', gave a good account of itself, and the 9.2 howitzer eventually became the British army's heavy mainstay. Observing its success, the designers offered a 15-inch which they had developed along the same lines as the 9.2. As mentioned earlier, the Admiralty took this weapon under its wing and sponsored its service in France, manning it with Marines, where it became known as 'Granny'.

In late 1915, finding they had enough to do without running a howitzer outfit, the Marines offered it back, together with some more which had now been made, to the army, who accepted the weapons, and now, for the first time, took official notice of them. The Ordnance Board, asked to comment, were forthright. 'This weapon was developed in such great secrecy that this is the first time we have seen it. Its range is insufficient, and we very much doubt whether it was worth the time and money spent on it.' However, they agreed to try and make something of it, and began work on a lighter shell which would improve the range beyond the 10,000 yards currently its maximum. But the new shell proved to be wildly inaccurate, and the Board dropped the project for something more important. 'Granny' and her cousins finished the war as they were, and were then honorably discharged.

Meanwhile the railway gun fever had spread like wildfire. Prior to the war, railway guns were a curiosity. The species saw its beginnings during the American Civil War and was toyed with by German and French designers during the closing years of the 19th Century. But it was the Germans who first made it a practical weapon, realising that with their internal lines of communication it was an ideal method of switching heavy firepower from one border to another for defence or attack. Britain had not shown much interest as there seemed little that railway guns could be used for in an island already amply provided with coast defence guns.

In practically every case the early railway gun models were standard naval or coast defence guns on a modified form of their standard mount, bolted down onto a suitably strengthened flat car of well construction, i.e. with the bed dropped between the trucks. Once in position, beams would be placed on the track and jacks positioned to take the weight from the wheels and springs for firing. With the

Above : German 28cm railroad gun. The box on top is a counterweight to balance the barrel and make it easy to elevate. The curved sections attached are to support camouflage netting. *Below :* The 28cm railroad gun opens fire

smaller weapons – six and eight-inch calibre – it was possible to mount the guns on racer rings so that they could be traversed about, though usually they were restricted to firing within a small angle of the track alignment so as not to topple over from the recoil. The heavier guns were permitted only one or two degrees of traverse for stability's sake, and had to rely on being pointed in the right direction to begin with. The French developed a system of making a curved section of track – named an *epée* – roughly aligned with the enemy target zone. The whole gun on its wheels could be pushed along the line until the curve brought the barrel into line with the selected target. The locomotive stopped, the gun was jacked up, and fine laying was done by the small on-carriage traverse.

The French were undoubtedly the greatest innovators of the railway gun business once the war started, and, although there is no positive proof, it seems likely that they were the inventors of the one device which revolutionised the railway gun and turned it from a cumbersome machine into a highly flexible weapon; the turntable. This, of course, was as old as railroading when considered as a method of turning a locomotive end-for-end, but its introduction as an artillery adjunct was of prime importance; so much so that after the war, when Krupp began to design railway guns for Hitler, he started not with ballistics but by designing a portable turntable.

But the very big guns were not suited to the turntable system, since they recoiled along the track when fired. Recoil is governed by the ratio of shell weight to gun weight – other things being equal. This explains why the Paris Gun recoiled in its cradle only for about five feet – it was a 210lb shell in a 142-ton gun. But the British 14-inch, for example, weighed 100 tons and fired a 2,400lb shell, ten times the shell weight and a one-third reduction in gun weight. This meant that some of the recoil force would be transmitted to the mounting and the whole affair would move back. This was possible in two ways; the sliding method, in which the gun wagon sat on steel beams on the track and slid back on recoil, the trucks preventing it slipping sideways; or the rolling mount, where you simply let the wheels take the firing shock and the whole gun trundled backwards along the track. There were two alternatives here; you could set the brakes or not. With the brakes set, the mounting would groan and squeal back a few feet. Without, it rumbled quietly back several yards. Either way, on an *epée* you soon ran out of alignment, and the locomotive had to come and push the gun back to the starting point. By careful tracklaying it might be possible to arrange for the gun to recoil uphill and then to trundle back under control of the brakeman after each shot. Another useful trick was to position it near a tunnel; fire a few shots which rolled you back to the waiting locomotive, hook up, and chug into the tunnel to hide from aviators and counterbattery fire. This trick was done by 'der Lange Emil', a 38cm German railway gun which shelled Dunkerque in 1915 at a range of about forty kilometres, and it was some time before the gun was located.

The Schneider company of France had done pioneer work on railway guns, producing a 155mm howitzer with all-round traverse in 1900 and a 20cm howitzer in 1910, both of which were stabilised by outriggers when firing, so as to take the recoil thrust entirely in the gun's recoil system. When the war came, Schneider were asked to produce the simplest designs of a heavy railway gun which would shoot, and were given a supply of ex-Coast Artillery guns to play with, of various calibres. These guns, although breech-loaders, were elderly designs which had been originally mounted on recoil carriages and slides; that is, when fired, the gun, attached to its carriage, recoiled bodily up an inclined

Above : British 60-pounders coming out of action ; the gunners crouch round the gun for protection while awaiting the arrival of the horse teams

Above : British 9.2-inch gun on railroad mount at the Battle of Albert, July 1916
Below : Admiral Bacon's artillery ; 'Granny', the 15-inch howitzer, being loaded near Arras, 1917

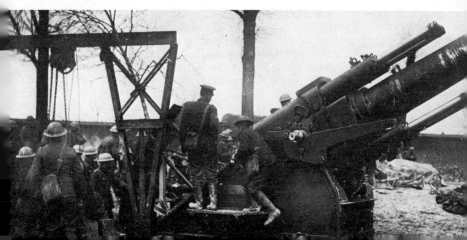

lane against the resistance of a hydraulic buffer. To mount such weapons on a field mounting demanded the design and construction of cradles and recoil system and enough has been said already on these complex devices to show that such a design job would have been no sort of short cut to having a gun in action.

So Schneider came up with an answer that was startling in its simplicity. They simply slung the gun by its trunnions into the side frames of the mounting. Once the mount had been positioned it was jacked down onto a platform of steel I-beams laid parallel with the track. And that was all. When the gun fired the recoil stress passed straight into the mount and was dissipated by shoving the whole equipment back along the I-beams. At extreme elevations the recoil was no more than a foot, at lowest elevations about four feet, on the 34cm version. After a few shots a winch was hooked up to the coupling on the front and the whole lot was dragged back to its starting point to commence firing.

Primitive as it was, the design was well liked by all who used it for the reason that rarely, if ever, did it need any attention. After all, there was nothing to maintain; no hydraulic system to be purged and refilled, no pneumatics to be charged, no glands to leak and be repacked. Now and then, after a few hundred shots a trunnion might break, but by that time the gun was almost worn out anyway. Not only were the old guns all used up, but new ones were designed to go on the same type of mounting and the vast majority of French railway guns were of this pattern.

Since most of the big guns readily available to the combatants appear to have been coast guns, it might be thought that with all the weapons being slung on wheels and rushed to war in France that the coast defences were being stripped. Nothing could be further from the truth; both Britain and Germany had extremely powerful navies – they had, after all, been a considerable factor in the political preambles to the conflict – and consequently neither side was willing to take chances on the defence of its dockyards and harbours while the Dreadnoughts were about. The guns which went to the land war were the 'reserve' guns, the spares manufactured in peacetime and literally kept on the shelf tagged with the name of a ship or fort to which they would be sent when the original armament was worn out or damaged. But the 'frontline' guns were ready on every coast, for the lesson of the Hartlepools had shown that a sea raid could descend anywhere at any time.

The Hartlepools stand cheek by jowl on the North Sea coast of England, and early in the morning of 16th December 1914 they were visited by three German battlecruisers which set to work to shell the towns. The two local coast batteries, mustering three 6-inch guns between them, put up a ferocious defence, but it was a one-sided battle with 104 ship-mounted guns of 15cm, 20cm and 28cm calibre ranged against them. Casualties to the civil population amounted to 112 killed and about 200 wounded, with seven soldiers killed and thirteen wounded. The 6-inch guns managed to kill eighty and wound 200 seamen on the raiders, as well as inflicting material damage, but the principal result of the raid was the realisation of the vulnerability of the coastline and the certainty that coast defence was not likely to be neglected for the rest of the war.

The United States, secure in the knowledge that the Germans would have to get past both the British and US navies in order to attack the US were able to thin out their defences both in guns and men to provide for the AEF as we have seen, but in Britain, with the threat only a few hours steaming across the cold North Sea, strengthening was the order of the day, and every port of consequence on the east coast was provided with

147

some sort of coast gun. At Hartlepool a sea mist had prevented a nearby battery from joining the fight, and where wide estuaries held out the possibility of such conditions occuring again an ingenious solution was found. To guard the waters of Spurn Head where the River Humber flowed to the sea and formed a wide lagoon, piles were driven into the seabed and two forts built in the middle of the estuary, so that even in the worst conditions any ship entering would have to run the gauntlet of these new defenders. In an attempt to reduce the weight and speed the building, a new type of 'sandwich' armour was proposed; two armour steel plates with a foot of concrete between. The Department of Fortifications and Works were undecided as to which of two types of concrete to use and requested a trials establishment to make a firing test. The test was done and the report submitted read, in part 'The armour is pierced completely by a four-inch shot at 9,000 yards range. It is to be hoped that the forts constructed of this material are never attacked.' The design was rapidly changed, the forts duly built and armed with 6-inch guns, and they remained in service throughout the First and Second World Wars without the new armour being put to the test.

In the north-east, Newcastle-upon-Tyne, with the immense Elswick Ordnance factory, innumerable shipyards and heavy engineering works and other war industries, was obviously a prime target. The existing guns were a collection of 6-inch and 9.2-inch, and something heavier was desirable in order to deal with raiders before they got close enough to use their guns. Enquiries were made to the US Government as to the possibility of purchasing 14-inch or 16-inch guns on disappearing carriages, but none were readily available and the process of manufacture would take a long time. So early in 1917 it was decided to take two existing naval gun turrets, of the type in the *Prince George* class battle-ships, each mounting two 12-inch guns and mount them in concrete at th mouth of the River Tyne. They wer to be carefully sited and their barrack and stores to be well away so as no to be easily seen from the air or sea with lavish protection of armour an concrete. After a good deal of dis cussion back and forth, it was even tually considered that it was not suc a good idea after all. The turrets wer cramped and the guns of an elderl design which prevented any great rat of fire being developed. If the job ha to be done, it might as well be don properly, and completely new turret designed to take the more moder and harder-hitting 13.5-inch guns This was agreed upon late in 1917 an work began once again. Eventuall the turrets were installed in 1918, bu the war was over before Kitchene Battery and Roberts Battery, as the were to be known, were completel operational, and then with 12-inc guns of a modern design. But all th work was in vain, for they were dis mantled in the 1920s without eve having fired a shot.

On the land front the war ha brought out the usual crop of inver tors of unusual ordnance. An earl contender was Colonel Sims-Dudle who advanced the claims of his pnet matic gun. It was little more than giant air gun and the inventor co veniently overlooked the proble of providing the necessary con pressed air; presumably it would hav had a compressor or, more likel relays of unfortunate soldiers woul have had to slog through the mt with cylinders of the stuff. The que tion never arose though, as the Britis army had been disenchanted wit pneumatic guns for some years, ha ing burned its fingers over the Amer can Zalinski gun in the 1880s ar having watched with interest tl performance of Sims-Dudley's batte of pneumatic guns in the Spanis American war, a performance whic moved them to decline the goc Colonel's offers.

In 1916 an invention was offered to the French government which had an interesting subsequent history. A gentleman named Fauchon-Villeplée decided to use electricity as the propulsive force in a gun. The idea was not entirely new, previous inventors having based their ideas on the soleoid principle in which the electric field generated in a coil of wire was used to expel the projectile within. Villeplée came up with something entirely new however: two bus-bars formed the gun barrel and a winged projectile lay between. By applying a current to the bus-bars the projectile was rapidly accelerated, and a two-metre long cannon propelled a fifty-gramme projectile with enough force to pierce eight inches of pine at twenty-five yards range. In fact, he had designed what is known today as a linear motor.

The French Commission on Inventions were not impressed by his figures and turned the idea down, so he went off, built his two-metre model, and in 1917 came back to try again. With a working device to prove his point, he got a hearing and the Commission was sufficiently impressed to give him instructions to manufacture a cannon firing a 5cm calibre projectile. This was in July 1918, and before the design was worked out the war was over and the contract was cancelled. Together with some companions, he then wrote a short book on his invention in which he was somewhat sharp in his observations on the lack of foresight of the French government in failing to appreciate the worth of his invention and not giving him suitable backing.

In 1944 we find the Luftwaffe plunging money into an identical weapon to be used as an anti-aircraft gun. This also failed to get past the model stage. Critical examination of the system by Allied technicians after the war revealed the flaw in the device – its colossal appetite for electricity. Villeplée's original figure for a gun to fire a 100-kilogramme shell demanded 7,000,000 amperes at 1,350 volts, and he was underestimating. The Luftwaffe's 40mm gun would have needed a full-size power station. The electric gun is still not with us.

The introduction of the tank in 1916 gave rise to several thoughts on the subject of using the caterpillar principle to move guns rapidly across country. Admittedly the tank moved only at a walking pace, but even this was rapid in the mud and shell-hole landscape of Flanders, which utterly defeated ordinary wheeled artillery. Probably the earliest attempt was the British 60-pounder gun carrier, a much modified tank chassis into which a wheel less 60-pounder gun could be winched. The wheels were hung on brackets on the side so that they could be refitted when the gun was placed in action, for this was a carrier only, and not a self-propelled gun. A few were built, but there seemed little point in the complicated and heavy exercise of removing the wheels, winching on and off and replacing the wheels when the gun could as easily be dragged to most places with an ordinary caterpillar tractor. So they were politely turned down by the gunners and finished up as supply carriers for the infantry where they were probably of more use.

The French were not slow to adopt the tank; Estienne, their principal supporter in the French Army, began with the idea of mounting the ubiquitous 75mm Model 1897 in an armoured box on top of a simple caterpillar chassis so as to get the gun forward in the attack where it could do a better job of support. Unfortunately the idea misfired, the vehicles suffered from poor performance and reliability and were unable to exert any influence when they were put in action at Chemin des Dames in support of Nivelle's ill-starred offensive. After this, the French turned to the light-tank concept and did no more development on the 75mm gun tank, but, leaping from one extreme to the other, once their two-man Renaults were in

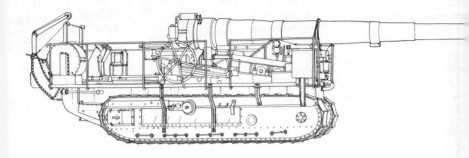

St Chamond self-propelled gun. One of the first self-propelled guns ever developed, this is the petrol-electric driven St Chamond 155mm gun. Power was supplied from a generator tractor attached to the front : the gun barrel points over the rear of the mounting

French St. Chamond Tank, mounting a 75mm field gun M 1897

An early US attempt at self-propulsion, this 8-inch howitzer was built by the
Morgan Engineering Co of Alliance, Ohio

Schneider self-propelled gun. The Schneider SP carriage was driven by a gasolene
engine in the rear end of the mount, while the driver sat up front, beneath the gun
barrel. The entire gun and its top carriage recoil on the mounting. As with the St
Chamond, the principal drawback lay in the limited elevation and hence short range

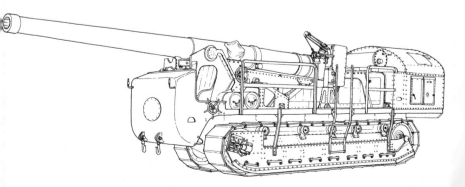

production, they plunged into a programme of tracklaying under such guns as the 155mm, the 24cm and the 24cm howitzer. Few were built and fewer still got into action; one or two were reported in the St Mihiel salient in 1918 with the American troops, and very little has ever been heard about as to what sort of performance they had or what kind of results they achieved. They were strictly what they set out to be, self-propelled guns, with no attempts at armour protection or pretence to a mobile fighting capability, things which have often blurred the edges of subsequent designs. Their object, as much as anything, was to reproduce a railway gun without the formality of having to lay rails, and one can only suppose that their limited mobility was sufficient for that.

Three models of which details are available show that considerable thought and design ability went into them. Two were developed by St Chamond and used Holt suspension with Crochat-Collardeau petrol-electric drive. A generator tractor carried a powerful engine-generator combination set which drove electric motors which drove the tracks. This vehicle was attached by a rigid drawbar to the gun carriage, also electrically driven and supplied with power through a flexible cable from the generator tractor. So the gun and its tractor moved as a linked train, controlled by the tractor driver, the gun carriage driver merely steering. On the gun carriage chassis the 155mm gun or howitzer were mounted, pointing to the rear, on mountings of the Vavasseur type in which the gun recoiled up an inclined plane against the resistance of a hydraulic buffer.

The Schneider 155mm gun was of more sophisticated appearance and was completely self-contained, a 6-cylinder gasoline engine at the rear driving the tracks mechanically through a gearbox. The gun faced forward over the driver's head and recoil was absorbed by allowing the

top carriage, supporting the gun, to slide on the vehicle carriage, controlled by a hydraulic buffer.

But the labours of the artillerymen were almost over now; from the minuscule beginnings of 1914, through the lean times of 1915 when guns and ammunition were scarce and fraught with peril, through the increasing tempo of 1916 with its barrages and gas, 1917 with its rethinks and reconsiderations, to 1918 with the artillery in command of the battlefields in fact if not in name. And the battles of 1918 were the flowering of four years of hard-won experience and an object lesson in the handling and deployment of massed artillery which was only repeated by the Soviet army in 1944 and 1945, and which is unlikely to be repeated again.

As 1918 opened, the German army had an undoubted numerical and tactical superiority over the Allies. While Britain and France combed their administrative tails to produce more combat troops, and while America intensively trained its raw recruits, Germany was able to withdraw experienced divisions from the Eastern Front, for Russian resistance there was now of little moment. Tactically too the Eastern Front was paying its way, for Bruchmuller and Hutier at Riga pointed the way to tactical innovations which looked as if they might well punch a gaping hope in the weakened Allied front and bring the whole sorry business to a precipitate end.

Ludendorff, now commanding on the Western Front, gave Bruchmuller the responsibility for preparing and planning the artillery support for the spring offensive, which was to go forward in March and April. Bruchmuller was particularly concerned with the attack on the British line from La Bassée to Armentières, an eleven-mile front which covered some dark and bloody ground and over which the British had bled unceasingly. For this was the Ypres area once more and there had already been three major battles there, carnages of mud which even today evoke bitter responses among Englishmen.

Ludendorff's master plan for the 1918 offensive was brutally simple. To throw a massive attack at the British Fifth Army near St Quentin, and when that obstacle was overcome and other areas weakened by the inevitable call for reinforcements, to launch a second attack on the Ypres area in the hopes of reaching the Belgian coast. Once these two strokes had concentrated all the Allied reserves and effort in the north, a third assault would hit the French Sixth Army near Soissons and drive for Paris.

To achieve this, Bruchmuller was given whatever he wanted, and he deployed over 6,000 guns of every calibre across a forty-mile front, one gun for every eight yards. The artillery bombardment was not to be the prolonged advertising campaign favoured by the Allies, but a hurricane battering of smoke, gas and explosive aimed broadside at every known British trench, communication centre, gun position, dump and headquarters. Once the necessary saturation was done, the guns were to switch to a rolling barrage to get the leading troops across to the British trench lines, and the fire would disperse again with the object of killing troops, wrecking installations and preventing movement of reinforcements within the area of the attack.

Under cover of the guns would come the infantry; but no longer in the extended lines which had become trademark of the Western Front. As the infantry divisions were assembled, their best men were pulled out and formed into storm battalions armed with light machine guns, the newly-developed Bergmann machine pistol, grenades, flame throwers – the accent was on close combat, fast movement, and irresistible firepower. Moving behind the artillery screen in close bunches, taking advantage of the ground and ignoring anyone else on the battlefield, they were each given an objective and how they got it was their own affair. Rarely has initiative been so officially blessed.

Once these storm troops were launched, reinforcements were to move up. Not on any prearranged plan, but into a general reserve area to await the call. The call was to come from the stormers when they had found, by their probing, a weak spot in the British lines and penetrated it. Then a party from the reserves was to go through the gap, fan out to take the surrounding positions from the rear, and that way gradually chop up the British line. The stormers meanwhile were going on; not for them the consolidation. Their task was to push on, making a gap for yet more reserves to be thrown in. And so the momentum was to be kept up; fresh storm battalions would be fed in periodically as the earlier ones tired or were decimated. The artillery plan with its accent on concentrations allowed gaps for the stormers to move through, and also marked out British positions and areas for them. But generally the idea was to try and move so fast that the artillery area would be left behind, the guns neutralising it and keeping the British so occupied that they would not be able to intercept the infiltrating stormers.

The British Fifth Army, under General Sir Hubert Gough, had no illusions. Intelligence reports had been amassing during the German build-up, and Gough knew what to expect. He knew that Hutier was commanding the German units opposite him, and he had carefully read an appreciation of Hutier's tactics at Riga, and at Caporetto on the Italian Front. He wasted no time in telling Haig that he was in a good position to be overwhelmed by numerical superiority unless he could be reinforced and his defences realigned to deal with the infiltration tactics. Haig, on the other hand, was convinced that the French were to be the target – if, indeed, there was going to be an attack at all. After much argument, Haig

**General Gough, Commander of the
British Fifth Army in March 1918**

finally agreed that the Fifth Army
might be attacked, but they were to do
whatever they could in the circumstances: which is a military way of
saying 'It'll be all right on the night'.

Gough did his best with his eleven
and a half divisions. He was loaned US
Army engineers to help prepare defences; he deployed all his tanks as
static pillboxes; he scattered 18-
pounders about as anti-tank guns; and
the Fifth Army dug and wired because
its life depended on it.

At 0440 hours on 21st March 1918
forty-one German divisions were poised against the Fifth Army, and another
fifteen against the British Third Army
on its northern flank. But that was
only a tidying up operation; it was the
Fifth who were going to feel the edge
of the axe. Bruchmuller's 6,473 guns
opened at 0440 hours with a crash;
for two hours they were to bring down
general surprise fire on gun batteries,
mortar positions, command posts,
telephone exchanges and bivouac
areas. The shelling was a mixture of
phosgene, high explosive and tear gas.
The whole area was swathed in a
morning fog before the bombardment

began and the gas and smoke merely
made the visibility worse. On the
British side 2,500 guns answered with
their prearranged defensive fire, and
the noise defied description. In the
middle of the preparatory bombardment, at 0530 hours, all the German
guns suddenly switched and dropped a
ten-minute intense fire on the front
line infantry trenches, by way of dis-
couraging any defenders who were
standing-to in the hopes of picking of
an attack. At 0640 the general
bombardment stopped and for half an
hour all the German batteries, in turn
fired check rounds onto the British
infantry positions. Then at 0710
having deduced fresh data from the
check firing, the bombardment opened
in earnest on the infantry, while
heavier weapons began shelling gun
batteries and dumps in the rear. After
half an hour, the pattern was varied by
the bombarding guns sweeping their
fire about, moving the fall of shot a
degree or two right and left and a
hundred or two yards plus and minus
of their assigned targets, so as to
collect any outlying sub-units or
personnel who had escaped the main
bombardment. At 0820 hours there was
a change of targets for the long range
guns, the infantry bombardment shif-
ted its pattern, but to the suffering
defenders it felt very much the same
as before. Finally, at 0935 the pattern
changed again; now all howitzers were
to fire as close to the front line as they
could; beyond them the *minenwerfer*
fired and beyond them the field guns.
The heavy and super-heavy guns were
to bombard the British second line,
though a large number of the heavy
weapons were continuing to douse the
British guns with gas.

While this all took place, the storm
troops rose silently and moved in to
their assault. At 0940 the whole
pattern of fire began to move forward
in the form of a barrage, first lifting
300 metres and halting three minutes,
then another 200 metres and a four
minute wait, and so on. If the forward
assault troops wanted the barrage

moved forward before the due time, they were to fire green rockets, but they were given no signal to request the barrage to be stopped. This was one of the most meticulously planned and fired bombardments of the entire war, and it did everything it was supposed to do. The British Official History records that 'the very air seemed to vibrate with shell-bursts' and the storm troopers slipped through the defences while those British who were still capable of thought were peering vainly into the fog and smoke and trying to discover what was going on.

Although the main body of the assault troops moved at 0940 hours, much discretion seems to have been allowed to local commanders in letting them get close to the British lines in the fog so as to have a quick run-in when the time came. Inevitably, blundering round in a featureless fog-bound waste led to disorientation and patrols intending to get close and lie up often found themselves involved in

The artillery rolls forward in the spring of 1918

small skirmishes with British troops as early as 0530 hours. By this date the German army placed little reliance on artillery fire to cut wire defences, and each storm troop party included pioneer troops to deal with wire and other obstacles.

The artillery assault was un-doubtedly effective, though the weather played a considerable part in making it so. In the first place, sitting in the fog, visibility never more than a hundred yards and often as little as twenty, made the defenders feel very isolated and vulnerable. The fog prevented signal rockets, to call for defensive fires from the British guns, from being seen. The shelling com-pletely disrupted all communications; even carrier pigeons were gassed. There was the added drawback of having to wear gasmasks for hours on end. The gunners, devoid of infor-mation, hard facts and target data, devoid even of rocket signals, and with visibility so bad they could scarcely see their aiming posts, could only engage their 'counter-preparation' targets, areas selected as being likely places for German troops to form up to launch an attack. By that time, however, the storm troopers had left those areas and it was largely a waste of effort. The 'SOS Barrages' in front of and surrounding Allied infantry positions were the next obvious targets to be fired on, but without visibility or communication, who knew when to stop firing the one and begin firing the other? Some of the heavy artillery batteries, steadily firing their allotted 'counter-preparation' targets, were only appraised of the true situation when infantry began retreating through their gun positions.

The result of Bruchmuller's devastating fire and Hutier's storm troops was to roll back the British army and cause heavy casualties. The front lines were swamped, and a serious loss was the high proportion of machine guns which fell into German hands, the lack of which was to prove critical at later stages in the battle. And the battle raged for a week before the battered and bleeding Fifth Army managed to hold the attack and establish a line. The Germans had won 1,200 square miles of land, about 1,000 guns, and about 90,000 prisoners. General Gough was relieved of his command, but postwar analysis showed that Fifth Army could hardly be blamed for the catastrophe which overtook them, and he was restored to favour.

Having set the cat among the pigeons, and with the Allies furiously shifting troops around to make good their defences against the German thrust, Ludendorff now looked at his next move, which was against the British First and Second Armies in the Ypres area. This had originally been planned as an attack on a thirty-six-mile front from Lens to Ypres, but since only eleven fresh divisions were available for reinforcing, Ludendorff cut his cloth accordingly and modified

General Erich Ludendorff; the Spring Offensive was his last chance

his original plan. The start was delayed by the necessity to amass the required ammunition, it being norma to build up twenty days' supply – a thirty or more trainloads a day before an operation, but for a variety of reasons trains were not getting through. Eventually the German Sixth Army was ready, aimed at Haze brouck, and the German Fourth Army were ready to exploit towards Messines, the ridge which the British had captured the previous July.

The British XI and XV Corps, who were to bear the brunt of this attack disposed their guns about a miserabl water-logged plain, concealing them as best they could. It had been an unusually dry winter in the area, an for once the ground was fairly firm i.e. not absolutely fluid. As well as th divisional field guns and howitzers the two corps had forty-eight 60 pounders, eight 6-inch and two 9.2-inch railway guns, 114 6-inch howitzers twelve 8-inch howitzers, fourtee 9.2-inch howitzers and two 12-inch howitzers. This sounds quite reason able, until one realises that across th way the German Sixth Army had bee reinforced to the tune of 105 field batteries, 206 heavy batteries, twenty-four super-heavy batteries, and six heavy *minenwerfer* battalions, and that this gave them an artillery superiority of about five to one.

The German bombardment plan was much the same as the one which had been so effective against the Fifth Army. Once more Bruchmuller organised it, complaining a little that he only had nine days in which to work everything óut instead of the seven weeks he had before. Once again fate took a hand and presented the Germans with a fog, and psychology also entered into the matter, because holding a critical position in the Allied lines was one of the two Portuguese divisions on the Western Front (the other one was out of the line, resting). This division was tired, awaiting relief, the men were none too cheerful and Ludendorff meant to take advantage of this fact.

The first German move was an intensive bombardment of Armentières - on the flank of the proposed attack – with mustard gas, a shelling which went on throughout the night of 7th April, swamping the town with almost 40,000 shells and causing thousands of casualties. The following day went by without a shot being fired, an uncanny stillness enveloping the whole front. Then at 0415 hours on the 9th the silence was shattered by the German artillery. Armentières received a further anointment with mustard gas, but this was only a sideshow compared with the storm of explosive and gas which was distributed over the defenders of the British line. As before, gun positions, communications, command posts, as well as infantry positions and trench lines were shelled. An additional refinement was the deployment of a long range railway gun which was employed to shell the British First Army Headquarters at Ranchicourt, many miles behind the line.

The bombardment went on until 0645 hours when it stopped for fifteen minutes to allow the gunners to get their breath, reorganise, break out fresh ammunition, and probably snatch a quick breakfast. Then at 0700 it opened up once more, this time against the trenches, wire and defensive works of the front line. But one feature of Fifth Army's suffering was not to be repeated: telephone and signal cable had been well buried, and except in rare cases was not broken, so that the defensive artillery was less blind. The British guns immediately opened up on prearranged targets which covered every likely German line of approach, but in spite of their prompt response the German attack moved off at 0845, their guns forming up to fire a barrage to shoot them on to the first defensive line.

The spearhead aimed for the Portuguese, and their three weak brigades were suddenly confronted with four fresh German divisions. The Portuguese were off to a bad start anyway, as one of the first shells of the bombardment had landed on their Divisional HQ and severed all communications, as well as upsetting everybody inside. But the descent of the storm troops soon proved too much, and in spite of valiant resistance by several isolated groups of Portuguese troops, the Germans succeeded better than they had hoped, and, by penetrating so quickly, soon unhinged the whole of the British front.

As the German attack struck deeper, splitting the British First and Second Armies, for simplicity's sake overall command was given to the commander of Second Army, Plumer. Plumer was a white-haired gentleman – he was known to his troops as 'Daddy' Plumer – who looked like the personification of Colonel Blimp and the dead hand of reaction. In fact he was one of the best and most astute commanders of the whole war, and at no time did he show his astuteness to greater effect than now. As the German attack went deeper, and as Haig issued his famous 'Backs to the Wall' order of the day, Plumer decided that the muddy, gassed, blood soaked real estate of

Flanders was no more than a status symbol, and a pretty poor one at that. It was not worth men's lives when some intelligent reorganisation of the line could shorten his defences, put him on ground of his own choosing, and by shortening his line allow it to be better defended by the troops available. So pull back he did, leaving a muddy waste in front of him to absorb and slow up the German advance. He was violently criticised at the time for apparently yielding up Passchendaele, Polygon Wood, Poelcapelle and other areas which had been won at enormous cost in 1917, but Plumer was a realist, and the truth eventually dawned on the others too. By shortening the line, he saved innumerable lives and also caused Ludendorff's attack to strike virtually empty space. It also brought the battle to an end, although this can also be attributed to Ludendorff failing to maintain his aim. Instead of sticking to his original and limited objectives, he was seduced away by his early success and tried to spread out to take in additional objectives, thus dissipating his effort. This dilution, plus Plumer's withdrawal and reorganisation, was to spell the end of Germany's efforts and marked the beginning of the end.

Ludendorff's final throw was his attack on 27th May against the French Sixth Army in the Chemin des Dames. Here, six French and five British divisions were taking things easy, thinking that all the activity in the north had drawn the German sting. They were wrong to the tune of seventeen fresh divisions of German troops, backed up by 3,719 guns. After a four-hour HE and gas bombardment which was every bit as violent as those fired in the previous attacks in the north, the storm troops poured in. Due to a certain amount of friction between the French general commanding Sixth Army and GQG, resulting in disagreement as to how best to defend the sector, the front-line trenches were packed with troops who were cut to pieces by the bombardment and

rapidly disposed of by the assault. Within four days the German army had advanced thirty miles, captured 40,000 prisoners and 400 guns, and had formed a huge salient pointing towards Paris.

The advance stopped at the Marne near Château Thierry, and one of the reasons it stopped was that the bridge was blown in the Germans' faces and the crossing denied them by the US 3rd Division, hastily thrown into battle. The Germans then veered off to Belleau Wood, but there met the US 2nd Division.

Now the tide had turned, and with

e French and American troops push-
g across the Marne and the British
my rolling in from Flanders, the
rmans began their homeward trek.
e need not follow them. The lessons
d all been learned by now, and the
lied guns simply had to apply them,
ing their multiplicity of calibres
d their prodigality of shells. At
59 hours on 11th November, a 155mm
owitzer of Battery E, 11th US
eld Artillery, in the Bois de la Haie
, the Meuse sector, very aptly com-
anded by Colonel Peace, fired the
st shell of the war. Having carefully
lculated the range to give the neces-

The Stormtroopers move up, following von Hutier's basic doctrines

sary time of flight, the gun was fired,
the shell looped away over the muddy,
bloody battlefields which had seen
the gunner's years of poverty, their
painful learning, their triumphs and
disasters and their time of superiority,
and eventually whistled to the ground
and detonated at one second to 11 am.

As the smoke drifted away and the
fragments pattered down into the
mud, all was quiet. It was over; until
the next time.

Bibliography

America at War 1917-1918 by Frederick L Paxon (Houghton Mifflin, 1939)
America's Munitions 1917-1918 by Benedict Crowell
Battle of the Somme by A Farrar-Hockley (Batsford, London)
Gas! The Story of the Special Brigade by C H Foulkes (Blackwood, London)
Journal of the Royal Artillery by various authors
Journal of the United States Artillery by various authors
Ludendorff by D J Goodspeed (Hart Davis, London)
My War Memoires by E von Ludendorff (Hutchinson, London)